NAHUATL THEATER

Edited by Barry D. Sell and Louise M. Burkhart

VOLUME I

Death and Life in Colonial Nahua Mexico

NAHUATL THEATER

Volume 1
Death and Life in Colonial Nahua Mexico

Edited by Barry D. Sell and Louise M. Burkhart
With the assistance of Gregory Spira

Foreword by Miguel León-Portilla

UNIVERSITY OF OKLAHOMA : NORMAN

Also by Barry D. Sell
(editor and translator) *Nahua Confraternities in Early Colonial Mexico: The 1552 Nahuatl Ordinances of fray Alonso de Molina, OFM* (Berkeley, 2002)
(coeditor-translator) *A Guide to Confession Large and Small in the Mexican Language, 1634* (Norman, 1999)

Also by Louise M. Burkhart
Before Guadalupe: The Virgin Mary in Early Colonial Nahuatl Literature (Albany, 2001)
Holy Wednesday: A Nahua Drama from Early Colonial Mexico (Philadelphia, 1996)
The Slippery Earth: Nahua-Christian Moral Dialogue in Sixteenth-Century Mexico (Tucson, 1989)

This book is published with the generous assistance of The McCasland Foundation, Duncan, Oklahoma.

Portions of Viviana Díaz Balsera's essay appeared previously in "A Judeo-Christian Tlaloc or a Nahua Yahweh? Domination, Hybridity, and Continuity in the Nahua Evangelization Theater," *Colonial Latin American Review* 10, no. 2 (2001): 209-27. Reprinted with permission. http://www.tandf.co.uk/journals/carfax/10609164.html.

Library of Congress Cataloging-in-Publication Data

Nahuatl theater / edited by Barry D. Sell and Louise M. Burkhart with the assistance of Gregory Spira ; foreword by Miguel León-Portilla.
  v. cm.
  Includes bibliographical references and index.
  Contents: v. 1. Death and life in colonial Nahua Mexico
    ISBN 978-0-8061-3633-2 (hardcover)
    ISBN 978-0-8061-6882-1 (paper)

  1. Nahuatl drama. 2. Indian theater. I. Sell, Barry D., 1949– II. Burkhart, Louise M., 1958– III. Spira, Gregory.

PM4068.7.N35 2004
897'.4522—dc22

2004048046

The paper in this book meets the guidelines for permanence and durability of the Committee on Production Guidelines for Book Longevity of the Council on Library Resources, Inc. ∞

Copyright © 2004 by the University of Oklahoma Press, Norman, Publishing Division of the University. All rights reserved. Paperback published 2021. Manufactured in the U.S.A.

Nahuatl Theater

Dedicated to Fernando Horcasitas, author of *El teatro náhuatl* (1974)
We stand on the shoulders of giants

Volume 1
Death and Life in Colonial Nahua Mexico

To pathfinders Arthur J. O. Anderson and Charles E. Dibble, for their editing of fray Bernardino de Sahagún's *Florentine Codex* (1950–1982)

CONTENTS

Foreword, by Miguel León-Portilla	xi
Preface	xix
Acknowledgments	xxvii
Part 1. Essays	
Nahuatl Plays in Context, by Barry D. Sell	3
Death and the Colonial Nahua, by Louise M. Burkhart	29
Nahuatl Catechistic Drama: New Translations,	
Old Preoccupations, by Daniel Mosquera	55
Instructing the Nahuas in Judeo-Christian Obedience: A	
Neixcuitilli and Four Sermon Pieces on the Akedah,	
by Viviana Díaz Balsera	85
Part 2. Plays	
Transcription Guidelines	115
The Three Kings	118
The Sacrifice of Isaac	146
Souls and Testamentary Executors	164
Final Judgment	190
How to Live on Earth	210
The Merchant	242
The Life of Don Sebastián	268
Appendixes	305
References	321
Index	331

FOREWORD

Fernando Horcasitas (1924–1980) and Nahuatl Theater

Miguel León-Portilla

New Spain's various forms of theater in Nahuatl have attracted the attention of a good number of researchers. Thanks to them we know that such theater owes its existence to the efforts of Franciscan friars. In some ways this theater came to take the place of the feasts and performances of pre-Hispanic times. Only a few years after the conquest of the Mexican metropolis of Mexico Tenochtitlan (now Mexico City), some Franciscans, with the invaluable help of their native assistants, chose subjects mostly from the Holy Scriptures and also from texts already existing in Spanish or Latin, then prepared scripts, had them translated into the Nahuatl language, and organized performances.

Accounts left by some Franciscan and Indian chroniclers recall how intensely the natives enjoyed such performances, which were usually held in the open air. I myself, as an eyewitness, can testify how in our time many people have similarly enjoyed attending the staging of one of these old theater pieces. The staging was put on by a professional, Miguel Sabido, and his company, which includes Nahuatl-speaking actors. The performance also took place in the open air, near the pyramid of Tlatelolco to the north of Mexico City; there have been other performances at the sumptuous Palace of Fine Arts in the heart of the metropolis.

We owe to the Franciscans Toribio de Benavente Motolinia, Gerónimo de Mendieta, and Juan de Torquemada the first vivid accounts of how these plays were presented, as early as the 1530s at places such as the same Santiago Tlatelolco or in the atrium of the cathedral of Mexico City. Their extant scripts, mostly copies of the original texts, are preserved at various archives and libraries in Mexico, the United States, and Europe and permit careful appreciation of the plots, dialogue, and other stylistic attributes of the plays we know today as pieces of this early theater. A very good example of what can be done is offered by this book in which seven pieces are rendered (some for the first time) in English, translated directly from the Nahuatl language by Louise M. Burkhart and Barry D. Sell.

The recent "discovery" of what may be the oldest extant original Nahuatl text of this genre, dating to about 1591—entitled "Miércoles Santo" or "Holy Wednesday" and published by Louise M. Burkhart—demonstrates that the field is open to further progress in the study of what is indeed the earliest form of Euro-Indian theater in the Americas (Burkhart 1996). The recording, translation, and publishing of some of these plays has a rich history, in which a very significant role was played by Fernando Horcasitas Pimentel, to whose memory the *Nahuatl Theater* set is dedicated.

Predecessors in Research on Nahuatl Theater

I will briefly recall some of Fernando's most distinguished predecessors in the field. Two Mexican scholars deserve particular attention. One is the well-known bibliographer and editor of several sixteenth-century chronicles, Joaquín García Icazbalceta (1825–1894). He wrote a well-documented study on this subject, "Representaciones religiosas en México en el siglo XVI," published in 1877, as an introduction to the *Coloquios espirituales y sacramentales* by Fernán González de la Eslava. García Icazbalceta also made several references to the same matter in his *Bibliografía mexicana del siglo XVI* (1886 and 1954). His contributions in this field called the attention of scholars to these compositions conceived as an instrument for the conversion of the Indians and as a genre within the literary productions of colonial Mexico.

Francisco del Paso y Troncoso (1842–1917) is the other Mexican scholar who made important contributions related to Nahuatl theater. He was well versed in the Nahuatl language and an assiduous researcher in the main documentary repositories of Europe. He was the first to publish the Nahuatl texts and his own translations into Spanish of five pieces of this genre (Paso y Troncoso 1899, 1900b, 1902, 1907). He also wrote "Comedies en langue nahuatl: Une petite vieille et le gamin, son petit fils," a paper presented at the twelfth International Congress of Americanists, held in Paris (1900a, 309–16). Thanks to Paso y Troncoso's publications, examples of Nahuatl theater became widely accessible for the first time.

Two North Americans who spent a large part of their lives in Mexico, John H. Cornyn (1875–1941) and Byron McAfee (1880–1962), also became attracted by these plays. In 1944 they introduced and published the Nahuatl text and an English version of a composition entitled "Tlacahuapahualiztli (Bringing Up Children)," preserved at the Library of Congress (Cornyn and McAfee 1944, 314–51). This play does not have, as several others do, a biblical subject. Its theme is the Christian education that is to be offered to indigenous youth. As noted by its two editors, to achieve its purpose, ideas and forms of expression in the play were derived from some *huehuehtlahtolli*, testimonies of the "old word."

To the same researchers is due the study and English translation of another play, entitled "Souls and Testamentary Executors." A copy is preserved at the National Library of Anthropology and History, housed in the Museum of Anthropology in Mexico City; an English translation was published by Marilyn Ekdahl Ravicz (1970, 211–34). This is another example of a play with a nonbiblical plot, as it deals with the misdeeds perpetrated by a widow, helped by the executors of her dead husband's will. Instead of ordering masses for his soul, she used the inherited riches to foolishly enjoy life.

Byron McAfee translated another play into English, also catechistical, but like "Souls and Testamentary Executors" of a nonbiblical nature. Its plot has to do with the avaricious dealings of a *pochtecatl* or "merchant" who loses his soul in punishment for his misdeeds. McAfee's English version of this play has been published by the same Marilyn Ekdahl Ravicz (1970, 99–118). To the same McAfee, in collaboration with the short-lived but well-known Mexicanist Robert H. Barlow (1918–1951), is owed the publication and translation of another production, *Un cuaderno de Marqueses* (1947), a good example of popular theater whose plot has to do with the conquest of Mexico.

Angel María Garibay K. (1892–1967), the chief exponent in contemporary research on Nahuatl literature, included indigenous colonial theater among his many concerns. To it he dedicated a whole chapter in his *Historia de la literatura náhuatl* (1953–1954, 2:121–59). There he makes a pertinent observation on how "it was not possible that the Mexicans, once they fell under the burden of the Conquest, would lose their [essential] nature. Being a people inclined to live in the open air, they required the constant presentation of various forms of spectacles in their feasts during the year" (1953–1954, 2:122).

Garibay continued his discussion on what he calls "the catechistical theater," describing the pieces published by Paso y Troncoso and others of whose existence he knew. Commenting on an article by Fernando Horcasitas, "Bibliografía descriptiva de las piezas teatrales en lengua náhuatl" (Horcasitas 1948), he states that "it is the most complete attempt ever done on describing the known materials in this area of literary production. Therein thirty four pieces are included there" (1953–1954, 2:129). If in his chapter on "the catechistical theater" Garibay could not encompass all of what is known today about this dramatic genre in Nahuatl, it is at least true that he offered a well-informed comprehensive synthesis of it, as well as some excerpts of his own translations into Spanish of several of those plays.

Theater in Nahuatl, in a different key, is exemplified by the piece edited and translated into English by William H. Hunter, *The Calderonian Auto Sacramental El Gran Teatro del Mundo* (1960). This piece was originally adapted into Nahuatl by the priest Bartolomé de Alva Ixtlilxochitl, a brother of the well-known Tetzcocan chronicler don Fernando de Alva Ixtlilxochitl. In his publication Hunter discusses the historical background, paying attention to the development of various forms of theater in New Spain and in particular to the genre known as *auto sacramental*, to which this piece by Calderón belongs.

In his appreciation of the work done by Alva Ixtlilxochitl, Hunter states that Alva "demonstrates good judgment in refraining from any attempt to render into Nahuatl the sonorous intricacies of the Calderonian verse" (1960, 150). Hunter acknowledges the considerable help he received from Garibay and McAfee.

I have mentioned already the name of Marilyn Ekdahl Ravicz. Although not a scholar concerned directly with the Nahuatl language and culture, she produced a book entitled *Early Colonial Religious Drama in Mexico: From Tzompantli to Golgotha* (1970), with an ample preface in which she also deals with the pre-Hispanic background and the colonial context of religious drama. She offers English translations of the versions prepared by Paso y Troncoso of "The Sacrifice of Isaac," "The Adoration of the Kings," and "The Destruction of Jerusalem."

She includes three more pieces in her book. These are: "The Merchant," "How the Blessed Saint Helen Found the Holy Cross," and "Souls and Testamentary Executors." In doing this she took advantage of the translations into English done by McAfee, who, according to her, authorized their publication. In only one case, that of "Souls and Testamentary Executors," had McAfee prepared his translation in collaboration with Cornyn. The main merit of Ravicz's book is its calling attention once more to the existence of this colonial literary genre.

The authors we have considered published their works years before the more comprehensive contribution by Fernando Horcasitas. Several of them profited from Fernando's bibliographical essay on Nahuatl theater that appeared in 1948. Here I will just add that, after the publication of Horcasitas's *El teatro náhuatl* in 1974, others have continued research on various aspects of the same subject, although—with the exception of Louise M. Burkhart (1996)—no one has edited and translated another piece originally in Nahuatl. The names and works of those researchers are María Sten, *Vida y muerte del teatro nahuatl* (1974, 1982) and Othón Arróniz, *Teatro de evangelización en Nueva España* (1979). They both continued along the lines first proposed by José Rojas Garcidueñas as early as 1935 in his *Teatro de la Nueva España en el siglo XVI*, in which no in-depth research was done to approach directly the compositions in their Nahuatl originals.

Fernando Horcasitas's Distinguished Career as a Nahuatl Scholar

Born in Los Angeles, California, on September 26, 1924, and registered by his parents as a Mexican citizen, Fernando grew up in an environment influenced by two cultures. In the milieu of his family he became rooted in Mexican tradition. While attending grammar school and later Loyola High School, he was at the same time exposed to Anglo-American culture. So it was that his background was bicultural and bilingual. He could express himself, with equal proficiency and elegance, in both Spanish and English.

When his parents returned to Mexico in 1944, putting an end to their voluntary political exile, Fernando settled in the country's capital. He then enrolled in the Department of Philosophy and Letters of the National University. There he became deeply interested in studies of a humanistic nature, mainly history and linguistics. Two years later he joined the National School of Anthropology, concentrating on the fields of ethnology, archæology, and Nahuatl culture.

At those two institutions he met Robert H. Barlow; it was an encounter that profoundly influenced his professional career. In 1947, at Barlow's request, he began to serve as secretary for *Tlalocan*, a journal of source materials on the native cultures of Mexico. Many years later, in 1977, he wrote in the same magazine an article entitled "Para la historia de *Tlalocan*," in which he described the origin of this journal, conceived, as he stated, by Barlow, "one of the most brilliant anthropologists attracted by the cultures of Ancient Mexico" (Horcasitas 1977, 15).

Under the guidance of professors as distinguished as Pablo Martínez del Río and Wigberto Jiménez Moreno, he obtained in 1953 his master's degree in anthropology summa cum laude. His dissertation, entitled "An Analysis of the Deluge Myth in Mesoamerica," was presented at the institution then known as Mexico City College, the predecessor of what is now the Universidad de las Américas. At the same college he began his teaching activities, which embraced a rather large number of subjects including the ethnohistory of Mesoamerica, the Nahuatl language, and a seminar on folklore narrative.

Among his first publications the one already mentioned on Nahuatl theater, published in the *Boletín Bibliográfico de Antropología Americana*, stands out, as it signaled the revival of active interest in this genre of Nahuatl literature and the beginning of Fernando's valuable contributions in the area. His activities as secretary of *Tlalocan* intensified following Barlow's death in 1951, and he took on the task of publishing the journal as one of his most cherished responsibilities until the end of his life.

In *Tlalocan* and in other journals such as *Mesoamerican Notes, Estudios de Cultura Náhuatl*, and *Anales de Antropología* he published a good number of articles, several of which dealt with oral tradition and theatrical pieces performed in some contemporary Nahuatl-speaking communities such as, for example, "Textos de Xaltepoxtla" (1962), "Los xoxocoteros, una farsa indígena" (1967), "El entremés del Señor de Yencuictlalpan, una farsa en náhuatl" (1972a), and "La danza de los tecuanes" (1980).

In 1963 Fernando Horcasitas became a full-time research professor at the National University. There he taught Nahuatl in the Department of Summer Courses. Becoming a member of the same university's Institute of Historical Research, of which I was director, he played a significant role in the creation there of a Department of Anthropology. The seventeen years he worked at the university, in particular those since the transformation of said department into the Institute of Anthropological Research in 1968, were particularly fruitful in his life. He prepared and published several other contributions while working there. Two had to do with oral narratives he had collected from a very distinguished native speaker of Nahuatl, doña Luz Jiménez (1897–1965), native of the town of Milpa Alta in the southern part of the Federal District of Mexico.

In one he presented the remembrances of doña Luz, expressed in Nahuatl, about the last years of the dictatorship of Porfirio Díaz and subsequent happenings during the Mexican Revolution of 1910–1920. Emiliano Zapata occupies an important place in her narrative. Horcasitas accompanied the Nahuatl text with a Spanish translation and an ample introduction. He asked me to write a prologue, which I did, stressing the significance of the publication. The book, *De Porfirio Díaz a Zapata. Memoria náhuatl de Milpa Alta* (Horcasitas 1968), aroused wide interest and was also published in an English version, translated by Horcasitas himself (Horcasitas 1972b).

Another contribution, also based on oral narratives by doña Luz Jiménez, was entitled *Los cuentos en náhuatl de doña Luz Jiménez* (Horcasitas and O. de Ford 1979). In it a good number of legends, tales, and other accounts were also presented in the original Nahuatl, accompanied by Fernando's translation into Spanish.

Horcasitas was very interested in the sixteenth-century work of the religious chroniclers and in several indigenous early colonial codices (books of paintings) with Nahuatl glosses. One manifestation of this interest was the preparation—in collaboration with Dr. Doris Heyden and with an extensive introductory study, copious notes, and an index—of an English version of what can be described as the ethnographic work of the Dominican friar Diego Durán, *Book of the Gods and Rites and the Ancient Calendar* (1971). His extensive introductory study is particularly valuable because of the information he gathered about the author and his work. Once again, Fernando asked me to prepare another prologue, which was for me an honor and a pleasure.

As for the codices, I will only mention two examples that had been previously unpublished: "Anales jeroglíficos e históricos de Tepeaca" (Horcasitos and Simons 1974), and "El Códice de Tzictepec, una nueva fuente pictórica indígena" (Horcasitas and de Magrelli 1975). The first is a pictorial chronicle with text in Nahuatl covering the years 1524–1645. It deals with natural phenomena held as omens, with epidemics, the arrival of viceroys, the building of churches, the execution of criminals, the construction of an aqueduct, and a plague of grasshoppers. The other document belongs to the group known as Techialoyan codices. It is interesting how in this codex there is emphasis on the bonds that the village of Tzictepec (near Toluca) had with Tlacopan in the period of the Triple Alliance and also during colonial times.

His Main Contribution

Busy as Fernando was with these and other publications, he continued his research on the subject he cherished so much: Nahuatl theater. In 1974 he succeeded in offering the first part of what he entitled *El teatro náhuatl: Épocas novohispana y moderna*.

As he put it in an introductory note to *Teatro náhuatl*:

The aim of the present work, of which the first part appears in this volume, is offering something little known to researchers of the language and culture of the Nahuas: a corpus of dramatic pieces in that language. We will take as a point of departure the catechistical productions of the first half of the 16th century, proceeding to those which continue to be represented in our towns. (Horcasitas 1974, 13)

In what is entitled "Preliminary Study" Horcasitas describes "the universe of the feast" and theatrical representations in several indigenous languages of the New World, particularly in Nahuatl. He points to what is known about pre-Hispanic representations, as one antecedent, and also discusses theatrical performances in Europe, mainly in Spain, during the Middle Ages and in the sixteenth century.

Concentrating on missionary theater he investigates its origins and purpose, giving also a chronology of its development. To facilitate an understanding of how such theater was staged he describes people's participation in it, the scenery and costuming, the music that accompanied it, and how the actors were chosen and taught.

Of much interest to the discussion in this volume is the attention he gives to the causes of the decline of this theater, as well as to the literary merit of the compositions, the reactions of the natives, and the results the friars obtained with these performances. The preliminary study, ample enough, is followed by an "Anthology of the Dramatic Pieces," in which he presents thirty-five of them, offering whenever available their Nahuatl text accompanied by a translation and a relevant commentary.

Fernando described in a "Note" at the beginning of his book what were the other dramatic compositions he intended to publish, in addition to those he labeled "ancient missionary theater," that is, the ones included as a first part in his published volume. The second part of Horcasitas's work should embrace pieces of moral content, dealing with themes not taken from Holy Scripture. A third part would be composed of the "Marian Theater," those about the Virgin Mary. Part 4 was to be dedicated to "Courtly Theater," also in Nahuatl, which would include adaptations from the Spanish classical theater. Pieces related to the conquest of Mexico and to the battles between Moors and Christians, and others in which the apostle Saint James played a key role, were to make up the fifth part. A last part was to be concerned with what he described as "Village Theater," a miscellaneous corpus of popular compositions, several of them still performed in modern times.

Of this vast project Fernando succeeded in publishing only the first part, dedicated entirely to missionary theater in Nahuatl. The materials he had assembled to be incorporated into the other five parts, in accordance with his plan, are preserved today at the Latin American Library of Tulane University in New Orleans, depository of his personal archives.

In the present book, three of the pieces published and studied by Horcasitas are rendered into English: "The Sacrifice of Isaac," "The Three Kings," and "Final Judgment." As to the other four pieces included here, Fernando knew about those published in *Tlalocan*, that is, "Yn Animastin Yhuan Alvaceasme" (Souls and Testamentary Executors) and "Yn Pochtecatl" (The Merchant). He was aware also of the Nahuatl texts that Paso y Troncoso had published and of others entitled "La Pasión del Domingo de Ramos," which is preserved at the Middle American Research Institute of Tulane University, and "La conversión de San Pablo," which was in a manuscript belonging to the bibliographer and historian Federico Gómez de Orozco. In addition, he listed and described, with the support of reliable sources, others pieces reaching—as noted—a total of thirty-five compositions.

Fernando Horcasitas Pimentel has left us a rich legacy of works related to the culture and language of the Nahua people. He guided and helped a good number of students and colleagues, and even when he had to interrupt his teaching activities due to illness, he kept his spirits up until his last days. Proof of this is provided by a report he wrote a few months before his final departure on the precise date of his fifty-sixth birthday, September 26, 1980. In this report he stated that he had reached the final stage of what would be the second volume of his *Teatro náhuatl*. He wrote also that "in view of the very poor situation regarding the publication of Mexican folklore texts and of serious studies on them, I plan to dedicate time to the publication of a collection of them" (Horcasitas in León-Portilla 1982, 36).

I just will add that it has been an honor and a pleasure for me to join here Louise M. Burkhart and Barry D. Sell in dedicating this book to Fernando's memory. He opened many new doors into the treasure trove of literary productions in Nahuatl, conceived indeed as a part of universal literature, produced by men and women of all times and in all places.

PREFACE

Louise M. Burkhart and Barry D. Sell

In the entire western hemisphere the only extant colonial plays in any Native American language are those in Nahuatl, the principal indigenous language of Central Mexico. In the decades following the Spanish conquest, Roman Catholic friars taught Nahua students to write their own language using the roman alphabet. As the Nahuas already had pictographic writing and tremendous respect for the written word, they enthusiastically adopted the new technique. European genres of discourse and text were transposed into hybrid Nahua-Christian forms.

As early as the 1530s, friars began to use theatrical performances as a tool of evangelization. Theater, like other performative modes of Christian devotion, appealed to the Nahuas, whose traditional religious activities focused more on collective rituals than on preaching or private devotions. A native theater developed, based on Spanish models but with native actors and sponsors. Scripts were authored by friars, in collaboration with literate Nahuas, and also by Nahuas themselves—with and without priestly oversight—and were sometimes based on Spanish scripts and sometimes invented for the local context.

The purpose of this and the other three volumes in the *Nahuatl Theater* set is to bring together and disseminate scripts and scholarship on this first truly American theater. By publishing a series devoted to Nahuatl theater we aim to establish the place of these dramas in the literary canon of the Americas, approaching them not just as an evangelization technique (as they have often been treated) but also as subaltern literature, as symbolic capital, as transcripts of intercultural dialogue, as primary linguistic data, and as artistic products.

We build especially on the work of the late Mexican anthropologist Fernando Horcasitas, whose *El teatro náhuatl* of 1974 is still the classic book on the subject. To this groundwork we bring a quarter-century of advances in the study of Nahuatl grammar and translation; current understandings of the colonial history of Mexico, and of colonial historical processes more generally; grounding in contemporary cultural and literary theory; and familiarity with the broader context of Nahuatl written expression, both civil and ecclesiastical.

The field of colonial Nahua studies has seen tremendous advances since the mid-1970s, with the publication of excellent modern grammars of the language such as J. Richard Andrews's in 1975, and Michel Launey's in 1979; the 1982 completion of Arthur J. O. Anderson and Charles E. Dibble's translation of the *Florentine Codex*, a Nahuatl-language encyclopedia of traditional Nahua culture produced under the direction of the sixteenth-century Franciscan fray Bernardino de Sahagún; and studies of Nahuatl civil and historical documents by James Lockhart, Sarah Cline, Susan Kellogg, Susan Schroeder, and others. This growing body of work has begun to approach (in sophistication if not in size) that done on early Euro-Americans.

Colonial religious literature in Nahuatl has not received equivalent attention, but significant contributions include Louise Burkhart's works (1989, 1996, 2001), Barry Sell's 1993 dissertation, Arthur J. O. Anderson's translations of some of Sahagún's doctrinal writings (Sahagún 1993a, 1993b), and Sell and John Frederick Schwaller's critical edition of a seventeenth-century confession manual (Alva 1999). Burkhart's *Holy Wednesday: A Nahua Drama from Early Colonial Mexico* (1996) examined in great detail one native-authored Nahuatl drama and its Spanish source. Similar work has not yet been published on other Nahuatl dramas; secondary studies continue to rely on limited sources and outdated translations.

Our volumes will bring the remaining corpus of Nahuatl dramas up to current standards of research. While the anthology format does not permit us to devote as extensive and consistent a descriptive attention to the texts as Burkhart did in *Holy Wednesday*, we engage the material at a similar level of intensity. We have made this a collaborative project involving scholars from different academic disciplines, in order to encourage a broader range of insights. Our work also complements and, we hope, will contribute to ongoing research by scholars in Mexico, such as the group working with Professor María Sten at the Universidad Nacional Autónoma de México, who recently produced a volume on Franciscan-Nahua theater (Sten et al. 2000).

The four volumes of *Nahuatl Theater* will include transcriptions and translations of all surviving colonial Nahuatl plays, some related Nahuatl texts, and scholarly essays by the volume editors and by outside scholars. We will use colonial-era scripts as much as possible. We will also avail ourselves of the copious material translated and composed by Faustino Chimalpopoca Galicia, a nineteenth-century Nahua scholar who was a speaker of the language.

Our transcriptions of the Nahuatl texts are meant to be useful to students and scholars of Nahuatl who need access to the dramas in their original language for their own translation studies and exercises. Our transcriptions will also support studies of language usage and variation across time and, to some degree, space. For example, linguists may use this extended corpus of documents to investigate Spanish influence on Nahuatl (use of loanwords, appearance of calques and syntactic changes), aspects of style (for example, the use of the reverential system, parallel constructions, traditional metaphors), and dialectical variation.

Our readable English translations are intended to allow both specialists and nonspecialists to understand the content of the plays and, thus, the wide range of dramatic themes and plots surviving from the Nahua past. How was life represented on the Nahuatl stage? How did playwrights working in Nahuatl go about their work? How were European texts and ideas adapted to the Mexican context? What multiple messages were conveyed by the plays? What staging techniques were used? Students of colonial social history and historical ethnography, of evangelization and religious history, of theater history, and Spanish American and Native American literature will find these translations a useful resource for investigating a variety of issues. Texts such as these should find an expanding audience among nonspecialists as contemporary Mexicans and Mexican Americans, including people of Nahua ancestry, increasingly seek to understand and recover their ethnic history.

These dramas speak to issues of multiculturalism not just because they come from another culture but because they are by nature multicultural, products of the hybrid zone between Spanish and Nahua cultural worlds. Theater too is by nature ambivalent, engaging two simultaneous realities: the imagined reality of the drama and the everyday world beyond the stage. Colonial dramas are particularly fascinating in that they display, in the microcosm of the theatrical event, the author's and actors' collective representation of what the colonial order is or should be, thus commenting on the "real" world. But this representation, presented in Nahuatl but stemming from European discourses, is never univocal but always conflicted and subject to different interpretations, native and other subaltern readings differing from those of the dominant Spaniards.

The project is organized into four volumes, of which you hold the first in your hands. A summary description of the individual volumes in the series follows.

Volume 1, *Death and Life in Colonial Nahua Mexico*, coedited by Barry D. Sell and Louise M. Burkhart, contains seven Nahuatl dramas dating roughly from the first half of the seventeenth century. Six of these plays have been previously published in now-outdated editions; one is presented here for the first time. Five are morality plays emphasizing death, judgment, moral reform, and punishment for moral failures; two are *autos* derived from biblical narratives (the story of Abraham and Isaac and the story of the three wise men). In the accompanying essays, Burkhart examines the plays' prominent themes of death and the care of the dead in the context of other Nahuatl writings on these topics; Sell examines the colonial social context of the plays and, through a close examination of the manuscripts, establishes their likely dates; Daniel Mosquera contributes a more theoretical piece on the plays' theological and catechistic aspects; and Viviana Díaz Balsera compares the dramatic treatment of the Abraham-Isaac story to its use as a moral *exemplum* in Nahuatl sermons. A foreword by Miguel León-Portilla, the senior Mexican scholar of Nahuatl literature, reviews the contributions of Fernando Horcasitas and other early scholars to the study of Nahuatl theater. A detailed discussion of the manuscripts—their present location, size, provenience, and peculiarities—can be found in the first half of Sell's essay.

In volume 2, entitled *The Virgin of Guadalupe*, we turn to the history of the Mexican devotion to Our Lady of Guadalupe, the country's principal religious focus. This devotion is the subject of much attention and controversy, witness the recent debates over the canonization of Juan Diego, the legendary Nahua hero of the apparition story, and the long historical debate over the authenticity of the apparition tradition. While the earliest (1649) Nahuatl version of the apparition legend has been published in a recent critical edition (Sousa et al. 1998), the later development of the Guadalupan tradition in Nahuatl remains little known, despite the central place this devotion came to occupy in native as well as nonnative Mexican religious life. Stafford Poole, C. M., one of the leading experts in the world on the history of the apparition, will be coeditor with Burkhart and Sell. Here we are concerned not with the historicity of the apparition legend but with its historical and literary development and dissemination.

Two colonial dramatizations of the apparition story are known. Nineteenth-century copies of both, made by the Nahua scholar Faustino Chimalpopoca Galicia, are in the New York Public Library. The first play, with three acts, is called *Coloquios de la aparición de la Virgen Santa María de Guadalupe* ("Colloquies of the Apparition of the Virgin Saint Mary of Guadalupe"); both Fernando Horcasitas and the Mexican scholar Ángel María Garibay Kintana attributed it to the early eighteenth century. A second and earlier copy of this play, made by or for the Mexican priest and scholar José Pichardo (1748–1812) in the late eighteenth century, is in the National Library of France. The other play, comprising one act in verse, is titled *El portento mexicano, comedia famosa, y la primera en verso Mexicano* ("The Mexican Portent, Famous Drama, and the First in Mexican Verse"); Fernando Horcasitas tentatively dated it to about 1690.

As companion material for the two dramas, in order to provide context on the Guadalupan devotion of the late seventeenth and early eighteenth centuries, we will include transcriptions and translations of some other previously unpublished Nahuatl Guadalupan materials, such as prayers and praise songs.

Volume 3, *Spanish Golden Age Drama in Mexican Translation*, on which the noted Hispanist Elizabeth R. Wright joins Burkhart and Sell as coeditor, will be truly bicultural, focusing on three Golden Age Spanish plays and a comic intermezzo (over seventy folios total length) that were adapted into Nahuatl by don Bartolomé de Alva Ixtlilxochitl around 1640. Alva's work survives in the Bancroft Library of the University of California at Berkeley. Alva was Spanish on his father's side but on his mother's side was descended from one of the Aztec Empire's royal dynasties. He was a native speaker of Nahuatl and one of very few men of either native or mixed blood to be ordained into the Roman Catholic priesthood. Thus, he was perfectly positioned to be a cultural broker between native and Spanish worlds.

The Spanish plays are *El Gran Teatro del Mundo* ("The Great Theater of the World") by Pedro Calderón de la Barca, the great master of eucharistic drama; *La Madre de la Mejor* ("The Mother of the Best"), about the conception and birth of the Virgin Mary, by Félix Lope de Vega Carpio, the most famous of all Spanish playwrights; and *El Animal Propheta y Dichosa Patricida Don Julián* ("The Prophet Animal and the Blissful Patricide, Don Julian"). A chapbook version of the latter play circulated under Lope de Vega's name, and Alva attributes it to him, but it was written by Antonio Mira de Amescua, a reasonably well-known playwright who was strongly influenced by Lope; this issue of authorship is itself of interest in studies of Golden Age drama.

An English translation of Alva's Calderón adaptation was published by William A. Hunter in 1960, before all the more recent advances in Nahuatl scholarship. The other two have never been published. This only known case in which classic works of the Spanish theater were rendered into Nahuatl provides a unique opportunity to see how metropolitan "hits," so to speak, played in the colonial provinces. The

Spanish plays, with English translations, will be presented along with Alva's work. This will allow the kind of controlled comparison between Spanish model and Nahuatl adaptation that Burkhart was able to carry out in *Holy Wednesday,* with an extra advantage in that we know the precise identity of the Mexican author.

In addition to their significance as local adaptations of Spanish masterworks, Alva's dramas are important for Nahuatl linguistic studies. Alva devoted his work to Father Horacio Carochi, the Jesuit linguist who produced the most important colonial grammar of Nahuatl (1645) and who developed a system for using diacritical marks to indicate long vowels and glottal stops, essential features of the language usually ignored by earlier grammarians. Intermittently, but nevertheless to a useful extent, Alva or someone familiar with Carochi's diacritics applied these marks to his translations. Our work will reproduce these revealing diacritics and analyze how they were used. In directing his theatrical translations to the Jesuits, Alva intended them for linguistic study and training rather than for performance since Jesuits ordained in Mexico were required to study Nahuatl. Thus while it is possible that Alva's work was performed, we do not assume this was the case and will treat the plays as having primarily been texts for private study.

Volume 4, *Nahua Christianity in Performance,* is still in the planning stages. We intend to include all other extant colonial and nineteenth-century Nahuatl plays, including a Passion play recently discovered in Mexico, works copied or composed by Faustino Chimalpopoca Galicia in addition to the Guadalupan dramas, and two pieces held by the John Carter Brown Library.

Our principal goal is to present the dramas with meticulously accurate transcriptions, up-to-date and readable translations, and supporting documentation on dating, authorship, and context. Our secondary goal is to offer interpretations of the historical, literary, religious, and linguistic significance of the materials through the supplementary essays.

The process by which a set of volumes such as this is produced and the general guidelines that are followed may be of some use to those interested in undertaking similar projects or in extending the work we have begun here. Briefly stated, they can be organized into five categories: identification of sources, establishment of authoritative texts, transcription, translation, and interpretation.

Locating and identifying sources is fundamental to our work. Much of the extant corpus of colonial Nahuatl dramas is fairly well established but surprises occur: the "Holy Wednesday" drama was discovered in 1986 and a Passion drama was recently discovered in Mexico. The original manuscript of three plays in our volume 1, lost according to some scholars, resides contentedly in the Clements Library of the University of Michigan; some other "lost" texts may also reappear. The text currently held by the Academy of American Franciscan History, "The Life of Don Sebastián," was unknown until very recently.

Establishing an authoritative text is often trouble free. In most cases, only one copy of a Nahuatl drama survives. However, one exception is a drama in our volume 1, for which a second copy follows the first in the Library of Congress manuscript. We transcribed both but translated only the first, noting all meaningful discrepancies in wording between that version and the second copy. Another exception is the

"Colloquies of the Apparition" Guadalupan drama, for which two versions survive. Using both versions in tandem, we will produce as authoritative a reconstruction of the original as possible, documenting the discrepancies between the two extant versions.

The issue is much more complex for the Spanish dramas in volume 3, as these circulated in various manuscript and chapbook versions before or alongside more "authoritative" editions. For our work to be a valid contribution to studies of Golden Age drama, we must give serious attention to identifying the correct texts. We are in the process of determining (from date and content) which of the extant versions of the Spanish plays were the likeliest candidates to have been used by Alva as the basis for his Nahuatl adaptations. These, rather than any now-standard editions, are the relevant sources for the *Nahuatl Theater* set. This task requires extensive archival research in multiple repositories: the National Library in Madrid, the Archive of the Indies in Seville, the Spanish theater archive in Almagro, the British Library, and the University of Pennsylvania Library.

Meticulous transcriptions form the foundations of accurate translations and interpretations. Working from originals or microfilms, we digitally transcribe the dramas. Transforming handwritten Nahuatl into digital format is always somewhat problematic, as scribes used various abbreviations, diacritics, and punctuation marks that cannot always be reproduced exactly. Some standardization of diacritics is inevitable, but we include all such features and mirror them as closely as possible. The orthography of the original is reproduced exactly. Following established practice, we do insert spaces between words and eliminate spaces within words (Nahua scribes tended to write in phonological units rather than words; line endings frequently bisect words). When one person has completed a transcription, another checks it thoroughly, marking corrections. A third—and in some cases, a fourth—complete check is also made. Some microfilms are clear enough that all features are easily visible. When this is not the case, transcriptions made from films are also checked against the original manuscripts.

The most accessible part of the primary sources are the English translations, and they have been prepared with the utmost care. The colonial Nahuatl (urban, written) of these sources differs substantially from contemporary spoken Nahuatl. Our collective translation experience from our work with other colonial texts and our familiarity with European religious texts provides the best preparation for translating these plays. Our procedure was that one person completed a draft translation. A second person went over it thoroughly and offered corrections and suggestions. The first person incorporated these, the second reviewed the text again, and a third person may also have reviewed the work. Passages that can be translated only tentatively have notes stating as much; alternative readings for ambiguous passages are also noted. The translations of the Spanish dramas into English will be a collaborative effort by Elizabeth Wright and Daniel Mosquera, with review by Burkhart and Sell.

No text, especially for those unable to directly read the original, speaks for itself. A critical part of presenting Nahuatl theater to a broad scholarly audience is to provide interpretative essays. These essays are not meant to exhaust all avenues of investigation but to elucidate the scripts from a variety of disciplinary perspectives and, we hope, to inspire further studies of them. Of particular interest are issues of translation; the negotiation of power and authority between Nahuas and the colonial church; colonial Nahua religious understandings and practices; issues of authorship, literacy, and text production; and Nahuatl linguistics.

None of the above would be possible without the difficult and groundbreaking work done by our predecessors, first the Nahuas and the priests who wrote the plays and later those who copied, rearranged, and commented upon them. Priest-grammarians of the later colonial period would look back—with much justification—at the first half of the colony as a golden age of Nahuatl written expression. No subsequent period could hope to equal the time when the most original, germinal, and innovative texts (including the plays) were created, but the present could be considered another kind of golden age, one in which a great deal of previous lore and knowledge has been reclaimed for future generations, native and non-native alike. If the period up to circa 1650 was the "Golden Age of Production" of Nahuatl texts, the time from circa 1970 to the present could be considered the "Golden Age of Recovery" of that rich and varied corpus. That such is possible for Nahuatl plays is due above all to Fernando Horcasitas, whose *El teatro náhuatl* (1974) was so many years ahead of its time.

ACKNOWLEDGMENTS

This volume and the entire *Nahuatl Theater* set were prompted by the generosity of Gregory Spira. While working in the Hispanic Manuscripts Division of the Library of Congress he spontaneously offered to provide Barry D. Sell access to the Nahuatl texts held there. He then provided photocopies to Sell of three of the plays presented in this volume. Spira also checked the initial transcriptions against their originals. No less helpful was making his apartment available so that Sell was able to visit the Library of Congress and see the texts for himself. Such an auspicious start encouraged Sell to seek out other early Nahuatl dramas and to think of a more comprehensive effort. With that idea in mind and the first few transcriptions in hand, he approached Louise M. Burkhart with a request and a challenge: would she like to dramatically extend the work she began in her standard-setting *Holy Wednesday: A Nahua Drama from Early Colonial Mexico* (1996) by becoming the coeditor of a large Nahuatl Theater project? She quickly accepted. This took matters from wishful thinking to practical reality. And it all began with an unexpected act of generosity.

The institutions holding the manuscripts that are transcribed and translated here are greatly appreciated for preserving and making available these unique texts. The Library of Congress greatly facilitated the examination of their three plays. The Academy of American Franciscan History graciously shared a previously unknown early Nahuatl drama in their collection and granted permission to reproduce it. The William L. Clements Library, University of Michigan, which holds three of the most widely known early pieces, provided an exceptionally clear microfilm and allowed us to publish the texts.

We would also like to thank James Lockhart for his thorough review of a draft of our translations, as well as John Frederick Schwaller and an anonymous reviewer for the University of Oklahoma Press for their helpful comments. Our acquisitions editor at the University of Oklahoma Press, Jo Ann Reece, saw this project through a lengthy review process with unflagging persistence and enthusiasm. We also thank our in-house editor, Marian J. Stewart, and our copyeditor, Pippa Letsky, for working efficiently and enthusiastically with a cumbersome, multi-authored bilingual manuscript.

Subvention funds for this volume were generously provided by the University of Oklahoma Foundation, the Department of Anthropology at the University at Albany, State University of New York, and the New York State/United University Professions Professional Development Committee.

Last, we make special mention here of the contributors to this volume: Miguel León-Portilla, Viviana Díaz Balsera, and Daniel Mosquera. They participated when this volume was just a hope. Their efforts and their confidence in our project are greatly appreciated.

PART I

Essays

NAHUATL PLAYS IN CONTEXT

Barry D. Sell

The readers of this first volume of the Nahuatl Theater set hold in their hands some unusual texts. In the entire western hemisphere, the only extant colonial plays in any Native American language are those in Nahuatl ("Aztec"), the language spoken by the Nahuas ("Aztecs") of Mexico. Their rarity is hardly unexpected.

Colonial Mexico was the one area in all the Americas where a large number of alphabetical texts in native languages were produced. This was due both to native precedent and to European encouragement. Unlike other First Peoples of the Americas, many Mesoamericans already had a tradition of recording information by making symbols on paper.[1] The prestige attached to traditional writing eased the transition from local to intrusive modes of record-keeping. The Spanish variant of Europeans had their own reasons for encouraging a familiar literacy. Businesspeople and administrators alike benefited from the assistance, collaboration, and guidance provided by literate Christianized natives.

Native youngsters learned to write their languages with the characters of the Spanish alphabet. As the critical target group of Spanish colonization, the Nahuas were the first to adopt the new writing tradition; by the 1530s the first extant documents in alphabetical Nahuatl appeared.[2] Mayas, Mixtecs, Zapotecs, Tarascans, and others would follow suit decades later. However, the Nahuas' early head start, greater numbers, and wider geographical spread gave them an overwhelming advantage even among Mesoamericans who were culturally predisposed to the new mode of writing. Thus it is no surprise that most alphabetical native-language texts from 1500 to 1800, not only in Mesoamerica but throughout the Americas, are in Nahuatl.

The sheer bulk of the extant Nahuatl corpus is impressive but largely unknown to the general public. Ten thousand printed pages, most church-related, are dwarfed by ecclesiastical manuscripts; one in a Mexico City archive has 888 pages all by itself. Larger yet is civil documentation, which in spite of its present mass is but a fraction of its original size due to the unsparing vicissitudes of changing times and circumstances. Like its counterparts in other Mesoamerican tongues, the Nahuatl corpus includes sermonaries, confessional manuals, books of Christian doctrine, testaments, land titles, civil and criminal proceedings, bills of sale, and so on. Size does make a difference, though, for it allowed for more variety, and among the items particular to the Nahuatl corpus are plays.

There is an inherent difficulty in presenting these dramas to a broad audience. Except for the obstacles posed by deciphering the idiosyncratic scrawl of hurried notaries, colonial texts in Spanish can be directly consulted with relative ease by those who know modern Spanish. Not so with Nahuatl. The gap between colonial and current Nahuatl is significantly wider because Spanish influence on it has been profound. Hence critical or skeptical readers—including the vast majority of modern speakers of Nahuatl—will in most cases be unable to verify for themselves the validity of a transcription, the accuracy of a translation, and the soundness of the subsequent interpretation and analysis. Helping to bridge that gap at the beginning of the twenty-first century is the function of the essays in this and succeeding volumes of the Nahuatl Theater set.

The Manuscripts

A brief review of the texts should help orient the reader. They are described in the order in which they appear in this volume. The Clements Library of the University of Michigan holds three texts bound together: "The Three Kings" (1r–23r), "The Sacrifice of Isaac" (23v–36r), and "Souls and Testamentary Executors" (36v–52r). A set of four bound pieces is held by the Library of Congress (LC): "Final Judgment" (1r–10v), two versions of "How to Live on Earth" (11r–28v [the basis of the English translation included here], 29r–43v), and "The Merchant" (44r–53v).[3] The Academy of American Franciscan History owns a previously unknown play: "The Life of Don Sebastián" (29 pages).

Long-established conventions for titling in Spanish and English have been followed in four of the seven cases. "The Life of Don Sebastián" is presented here for the first time. One of the two translators of this piece, Louise M. Burkhart, chose the title from the opening words of the main text, "Moral example which speaks about the life of Don Sebastián" (p. 5). "How to Live on Earth" was originally presented by John H. Cornyn and Byron McAfee in *Tlalocan* 1.4 (1944) as "Tlacahuapahualiztli (Bringing Up Children)." Burkhart decided that the present title, derived from an early speech in the play, would be more appropriate. "The Three Kings" was presented in transcription and translation first by Francisco del Paso y Troncoso in his *Biblioteca Náuatl* II (1900b) and later by Fernando Horcasitas in his *El teatro náhuatl* (1974, 256–79). Both of these noted Mexican scholars referred to it as "La adoración de los reyes." In the absence of anything resembling a title at the beginning of the drama, both editors think the present designation is more in accord with the opening lines.

Fundamental to analyzing these dramas is the task of establishing their authorship, dates of composition or copying, and provenience. There are several scattered clues to these pressing concerns. Prefatory remarks in "The Merchant" indicate that what follows is an

Edifying example that speaks about a merchant. I am writing it today; it is my property. My name is Don Joseph Gaspar and I am a resident here in San Juan Bautista Tollantzinco. I am setting down the day and year: today is Saturday, 15 November, of the year 1687. (36r)

There are later references to the *altepetl*[4] of Xochimilco and Tepeyacac, and to purchasing land "three years ago in the year 1627" (48r–v).

Also helpful is the following from the end of "The Sacrifice of Isaac":

Finis. Laus Deo. This moral example was prepared in the year 1678. It was copied today, Friday, the first of February of the year 1760. And as to whether in truth I worked on this moral example, [I affix my signature]: Bernabé Vázquez. (36r)

Some useful information can be found as well in "The Life of Don Sebastián." The first words read "Praise Play in Nahuatl" and "From Huaxtepec" (1). Near the end are the following remarks: "Finis. Laus Deo. Amen. This moral example was finished today, the first of April of the year one thousand, six hundred, ninety and two" (27).

There is no overt indication of whether the plays are Nahua translations of Spanish or Latin pieces or simply ad hoc creations composed by some combination of clerics and literate Nahuas. The two named individuals are little known. If Bernabé Vázquez was indeed the copyist of "The Sacrifice of Isaac," then he can be assigned the same role regarding "Souls and Testamentary Executors" since both are bound together and are in the same hand. He was most probably a Nahua notary, given his practiced hand and facility in the language, although his names were not the Spanish appellations most common among Nahuas. His status could not have been very high because he lacked the (by then) increasingly common "don."

Sporting the title when it had a more lofty connotation was don Joseph Gaspar of San Juan Bautista Tollantzinco who claimed to have written, or finished writing, "The Merchant" on Saturday, November 15, 1687. The references cited above to "three years ago in the year 1627" and to Xochimilco and Tepeyacac (most likely the *altepetl* of the same names that neighbored Mexico City to the south) put the play in a time and place I consider more propitious for its creation, that is, in the capital when Franciscan scholarship was at the height of its influence during the sixteenth and early seventeenth centuries. It should be added that Franciscans ministered to Tollantzinco (Spanish *Tulancingo*) and Xochimilco. Don Joseph was almost certainly not the writer nor even the copyist; colonial conventions called for the author of record, patron, or supervising editor to take full credit for producing a text.

Additional considerations point to a less direct role by don Joseph. In two notarial documents from Tollantzinco dated October 7, 1687, and Wednesday, November 3, 1687, don Joseph Gaspar appears as a witness, his formal authority deriving from his position as an *alcalde* or member of the Hispanic-style town council.[5] As with so many other Tollantzinco records, the notary of the *cabildo* (Spanish-style town council), don Joseph de la Cruz, wrote the entire text and apparently signed for everyone. Don Joseph Gaspar did not sign his own name, nor did he add his own distinctive rubric. The notary simply added the very same undistinguished rubric to don Joseph's and several other names. This does not prove that don Joseph was unable to write, but it does not speak well for the possibility.

The dates support my working assumption that all the plays have been through a process similar to that which produced two copies of "How to Live on Earth," each in a different hand and with a similar, though not identical, content.[6] "The Merchant" was created or copied in 1630 and then (re)copied on Saturday, November 15, 1687.[7] "The Sacrifice of Isaac" is explicitly said to have been copied on Friday, February 1, 1760, from a 1678 version that itself may have been derived from an even earlier text. The same dates may also apply to one of its two companion dramas ("Souls and Testamentary Executors") since it is in the same hand and literary style. The seventeenth century surfaces also in "The Life of Don Sebastián," which was finished on April 1, 1692.

Miscellaneous clues from "The Life of Don Sebastián" strengthen the church connection but leave the place of composition or copying still undetermined. The proclamation at the beginning, that what follows is a "Praise Play in Nahuatl," strikes me as a typically clerical formulation. Nahuas had infrequent occasion to speak of their cultural or ethnic entirety in terms of "Nahuas" (for the people) and "Nahuatl" (for the language) in texts written by and for themselves. Clerics had rather more, so these terms are usually found in ecclesiastical Nahuatl texts (see Sell 1993, 129–36). Unfortunately for our purposes, the names of early Mexican *altepetl* sometimes repeat, so it is unclear just which "Huaxtepec" is referred to on the first page of "The Life of Don Sebastián."[8]

Hence, little is securely known about such basics as dates of composition or copying. Previous scholarship on Nahuatl theater has at times erroneously indicated more secure dating of texts than is actually possible, and inherited errors continue to plague the study of these dramas. A pointed example is provided by something as simple as the dating of "Final Judgment." Fernando Horcasitas asserts (1974, 564) that in contrast with many other works described in his collection, "de *El juicio final* sí poseemos un manuscrito antiguo . . . fechado 1678 (aunque seguramente ésta es la fecha de la copia solamente)" (concerning *Final Judgment* we do indeed possess an ancient manuscript . . . dated 1678 [although surely this is only the date of the copy]). Until recently I myself thought the same (Sell 1988, 4).[9] Put simply: "Final Judgment" is undated, and there is no overt sign of any kind that it was newly composed or translated, an original or a copy.[10]

Proceeding, then, with caution, I turn to a consideration of some revealing aspects of the plays. These include the writing habits of the scribes, the types of loanwords present, the nature of the Nahuatl sociopolitical terminology used, and the pervasive if somewhat uneven presence of traditional Nahuatl formal speech.

It often seems that nothing that originated in the Spanish-speaking world remained completely unchanged once the Nahuas made it their own. The art of writing Nahuatl with the Roman characters of the Spanish alphabet is no exception. Yet even specialists in Nahuatl studies can little appreciate much of the strongly Nahua cast of the plays under consideration. James Lockhart regards Fernando Horcasitas's *El teatro náhuatl* as

> a vast contribution to Nahuatl philology . . . [that] brings together a substantial portion of the existing theatrical corpus in transcription and Spanish translation,

some of it published in the late 19th and early 20th centuries by Paso y Troncoso, and some of it published for the first time. As Horcasitas realized, TN is far from definitive. The transcriptions mainly modernize the orthography, with consequent loss of distinctions, although some idiosyncrasies of the originals are retained; division into words is often highly inconsistent, punctuation is arbitrary, and typographical errors and misreadings are rife. Horcasitas' texts are sufficient for many purposes, and for the most part I have used them without further recourse to the originals (which are themselves nearly all posterior copies, some of them unreliable modern transcriptions). The translations improve on their predecessors and give a generally adequate notion of the content, but errors abound, and much improvement is needed. In due course an updated, more complete, and much more critical edition of the corpus will be required. (1992, 595–96 no. 97)

The present critical edition attempts to build on the strengths of Horcasitas's work and rectify its weaknesses. The editors had access to the colonial originals of the seven texts in this book and used them as the basis of our final transcriptions.[11] We strenuously attempted to reproduce as far as possible all the original spelling, punctuation, and capitalization[12] although spacing follows current practices.[13] Consequently there are thousands of differences between the present transcriptions and those published earlier. Yet in fairness to Horcasitas and others, the reader should understand that these latest productions are no more sacrosanct than their predecessors. There are inevitable divergences between any handwritten manuscript and its modern typographic variant, in part due to the preferences and training of the transcribers. Future presentations of the same materials may include complete photoreproductions of the originals (not possible here), or utilize information technologies currently unavailable. Nonetheless the present transcriptions are enough of an advance over former renderings and are sufficiently suggestive of the originals that they supersede all previous versions. If nothing else, this latest round of transcriptions may encourage more direct personal examination of the texts. The editors would welcome that increased interest and scrutiny.

A direct comparison of transcriptions will help to demonstrate the contrast between the present renditions and earlier ones. Some of the spacing between lines has been adjusted to allow for easier reading of both selections. Horcasitas's version of "Juicio Final" begins :

JESÚS
Nexcuitilmachiotl motenehua Jucio Final
I
Tlapitzaloz. Motlapoz ilhuicac. Hualmotemohuiz San Miguel.

San Miguel: Dios itlachihualtzitzihuané, ma xicmatican inhuan ca tel ye anquimati, ca ipan ca in iteotenehuatiltzin in totecuyo Dios, ca quimotlamilliz, quimopolhuiz, in oquimochihuilitzino in itlazomahuiztatzin Dios in cenmanahuactli. Ca quimopolhuiz, quimotlamilliz, in ixquich in oquimochihuilitzino, in nepapan totome, i nepapan yoyolime, ihuan in amehuantin. ¡Ca namechmopolhuiz, in ancemanahuactlaca! (Horcasitas 1974, 568)

Our rendering of the same text from f. 1r of the LC manuscript:

+

Nexcuitilmachiotl. motenehua Juiçio final—
tlapitzalos motlapoz yIħ.^{c} hualmotemohuiz S.^{n} mig.^{l} =

S.^{n} miguel = v̄ Dios ytlachihualtzitzinhuane. ma xicmatican. yhuan Ca tel ye anquimati. Ca ypan Ca yn iteotenahuatiltzin ȳ tt.^{o} D.^{s} Ca quimotlamilliz quimopo^{l}huis yn oquimochihuilitzino. yn itlaçomahuiztatzin Dios. ȳ Senmanahuactli. Ca quimopolhuis. quimotlamilliz. yn ixquich yn oquimochihuilitzino. ȳ nepapan totome. y nepapā yoyolime. yhuan yn amehuantin. Ca hamechmopolhuis. yn ansemanahuac tlaca.

There are many noticeable differences in just these two small samples. More relevant to our purposes than the substitution of *JESÚS* for a cross is that Horcasitas added accent marks where there were none, drastically changed formatting, transformed notarial markings into a colon, resolved standard abbreviations, imposed current notions of capitalization and punctuation to create sentences, regularized most spelling according to his own lights, and added textual divisions (scenes) that did not exist in the original. Elsewhere he forces blocks of text into paragraph form. His changes conformed to the scholarly standards of his time and place, yet it is precisely the deviations from European-style norms that are of interest here. His "corrections" go a very long way toward eliminating precisely those features typical of Nahuatl documents.

Consider simply one aspect of the changes in punctuation. When left to their own devices Nahuas applied alphabetical writing to the elements discernible in speech—that is, letter/sound segments, syllables, and the phonological phrase—rather than to the European-style units of word, sentence, and paragraph with their relatively standardized spellings, punctuation, and spacing. Lockhart has accurately noted that the phonological phrase "consisting of a nuclear nominal or verbal stem with its affixes and its adverbial or other modifiers, is a far more obvious, detectable entity in Nahuatl than either the 'word' or the complete utterance (sentence)" (1992, 338–39). He later adds that, while the use of spaces to indicate phonological phrases is debatable, it is undeniable that in some instances Nahua writers used "a period (a dot at least) between phrases" and that this clearly shows their tendency "to think in terms of a phrase type quite foreign to European languages" (1992, 339). I concur. This clue to the identity of the writer is obscured in Horcasitas's version, and obvious in the present one.[14]

Certain features of the seven plays (eight texts) are now more readily apparent. Overall, there is intrusive *n* as well as the loss of *n* in all the expected environments; idiosyncratic capitalization that sometimes appears patterned; heavy punctuation in one part of a text that is seemingly abandoned in another; an indifference at times to the notion of standardized spelling; the presence of assimilation, loss, and gemination that might provide clues to the speech habits of the scribes;[15] the frequent use of *y* rather than *i* at the beginning of a phrase; and so on. All this within the framework of great variance among the texts. If I were to place the texts on some sort of continuum, it would go from those produced more independently by Nahuas to those generated under clerical supervision. Somewhat impressionistically, I would place the two copies of "How to Live on Earth," "Final Judgment," and "The Life of Don Sebastián" on the more independent end of the spectrum, the other four on the more supervised.

Nonetheless all the texts occasionally but persistently defy easy assumptions. Judging by the handwriting, six of the eight documents are by different scribes; only "The Sacrifice of Isaac" and "Souls and Testamentary Executors" come from the same well-trained hand. Yet all eight are in what I judge to be more or less skillfully rendered variants of the clear italianate hand taught by Franciscan *nahuatlatos* (experts in Nahuatl; translators) to their Nahua pupils in the first decades after the conquest. In some respects, such as the standardization of spellings, the two aforementioned plays hew more closely to European norms than almost any of the others. But then there is a distinctive anomaly, like their very nonstandard rendering of Nahuatl *ceppa* (in *oc ceppa* "again") as *cecppa*, with its outrageously impossible-to-pronounce consonant cluster *cpp*.[16] Such similarities and anomalies are to be expected from the general run of civil and ecclesiastical Nahuatl texts.

The original lettering tentatively provides additional clues to dating. Very early in the development of alphabetical Nahuatl writing there was some hesitation about how to represent the affricate [tˢ]. By mid-sixteenth century the digraph *tz* became the settled convention in most Nahuatl writings, especially those associated with the church. Alternative solutions from an earlier period of evolving standards are infrequent. Among the early manuscripts and imprints that contain such alternates is the anonymously authored Dominican *Doctrina cristiana* of 1548. The handwritten copy that provided the basis of the book was already rather dated because the by-then-dominant *tz* is a rarity in this book of Christian doctrine (for one of the few examples, see f. 13v). It is written variously *c*, *tc*, and *tç*, the latter two predominating (see ff. 6v, 11v, 30r, 124v, 129r, and passim; it is possible that *tc* is a print-shop error for *tç*). An even earlier Nahuatl text from circa 1540 uses *ç* and *z* in place of *tz* (Cline 1993). There are occasional later examples.[17] None of these notably early or nonstandard forms replaces *tz* in any of the plays in this volume.[18]

During much of the sixteenth century prevocalic [w] was variously represented as *v*, *u*, and *hu*.[19] A sampling from the mid-sixteenth century contains the following representative examples: *yvan/yuan, civatl/çivatl, peua, yehuatzin, vecauh, vel/uel, cavitl*, and *quavitl/quauitl* (Sell and Kellogg 1997, 341–49; *Doctrina cristiana* 1548). By the end of the sixteenth century, *hu* became the prevailing standard, again especially in church-related texts. Hence such items as *yvan/yuan* usually would be spelled *yhuan, vel/uel* as *huel*, and *quavitl/quauitl* as *quahuitl*.[20] There are thousands of instances where prevocalic [w] appears before *a*, *e*, and *i* in the eight pieces. With only one exception, there is always *hua*, never *va* or *ua*; always *hue*, never *ve* or *ue*; always *hui*, never *vi* or *ui*.[21] The relentless representation of prevocalic [w] as *hu* and [tˢ] as *tz* establishes beyond reasonable doubt that whatever the plays' original dates of composition, their extant versions cannot be earlier than the last quarter of the sixteenth century.

Another period-specific change occurred during the last quarter of the following century. Orthographic *s* began to appear where *z* would earlier have been expected.[22] Narrowing the possible environments down to that of verbal complexes yields results that are both expected and unexpected. "The Life of Don Sebastián," with its self-admitted dating of April 1, 1692, has *s* for *z* in 61 unspoken (i.e., stage and other directions) and 229 spoken (i.e., speaking parts) instances. This will serve as a baseline for what follows. "Final Judgment" has been touted to be very old but it has 62 unspoken and 110 spoken instances, fixing the present copy at a time probably no earlier than the late seventeenth century. A mild surprise is offered by "The Three Kings." Its traditional language is much too old for a late-seventeenth- or early-eighteenth-century date of composition, yet it contains 73 unspoken and 125 spoken instances. This speaks directly to the diachronic layering of the plays with their complex mix of features from different periods. "The Merchant" contains four unspoken and one spoken instances of *s* for *z*. Since I take it to be a 1687 copy of a 1630 text, this strongly indicates that the earlier date is the more operative one. In this case, the scribe copied fairly exactly an older text with spelling that probably differed from his, a practice that is reflected in some of the other plays in this volume. Between "Souls and Testamentary Executors" and "The Sacrifice of Isaac," there is exactly one unspoken instance of *s* for *z* in a verbal complex. Both texts were apparently copied in 1760 from 1678 versions, which themselves were surely much older, given the type of Nahuatl used. A real surprise is the first version of "How to Live on Earth." Here there are five unspoken and no spoken instances, all in a hand different from that of the main text. This and other features would place it sometime during the first half of the seventeenth century rather than the eighteenth as I had thought at first. This also highlights the differences I have observed between those parts of the eight texts intended for and worked on by scribes, the unspoken written instructions, and those shared by all members of the community, the spoken dialogues. Nonspoken parts tend to have more later-colonial features.

The above evidence suggests the seventeenth century as a central point around which the texts were composed or copied. This holds true as well for the types of loanwords present in the seven plays. Some years ago, Frances Karttunen and James Lockhart pointed out the diachronic patterning of loan acquisitions in their *Nahuatl in the Middle Years: Language Contact Phenomena in Texts of the Colonial Period* (1976). Subsequent work has refined and supported their initial judgments (see especially Karttunen 1982, 1985; Lockhart 1992, ch. 7, 1999, ch. 8).

They postulate three stages of Nahuatl's relationship and reaction to Spanish. Stage 1 was very brief. It lasted from Spanish contact to circa 1540. During this time, routine daily contact between the great mass of Nahuatl- and Spanish-speakers was almost nonexistent. Hence meaningful direct verbal communication was severely constrained because both sides lacked the requisite language skills. Only a tiny number of Spanish nouns were borrowed. Stage 2 lasted from approximately 1540 to 1650. This was a time of significantly more interaction between selected individuals and groups, leading to a greater capacity on both sides to communicate orally with each other. The overwhelming result was the passage of many Spanish nouns into the Nahuatl lexicon. These newly acquired items were accommodated to Nahuatl speech habits and they supplemented rather than displaced native vocabulary. There were also a few scattered anticipations of what was to come. Stage 3 begins circa 1650 and continues to the present day. A whole range of significant adaptations to Spanish occurred: unfamiliar sounds were acquired; a strategy for borrowing verbs devised; particles incorporated; Nahuatl syntax altered; portions of the native lexicon displaced; and idioms more readily adopted. These changes flowed from a deepening one-on-one interaction that had created a critical mass of bilingual Nahuas who served as a conduit for bringing more of the Spanish-speaking world into Nahua life. My own extensive reading of colonial Nahuatl writings confirms this schema.[23]

The seven translated dramas in this volume contain over two hundred Spanish and Latin phrases and words. There are a number of possible stage 3 items or features in the unspoken sections. The most notable is the Nahuatlized Spanish verb *trasladar* (to copy) in "omotrasladoro" at the end of "The Sacrifice of Isaac" (see f. 36r). However, I consider the central and more resistant-to-change original core of the plays to be that which the actors spoke and the audience heard—that is, the dialogues. There the picture is quite different. The loans shrink drastically in half, to 111. There are no examples of borrowed verbs using the Nahuatl verbalizing suffix *-oa* (see above). There are none of the Spanish particles used by post-1650 Nahua writers such as *sin, como, para, hasta, pero,* and *mientras*. There are no Spanish-style dependent clauses introduced by the Spanish particle *que* or by its back translation into Nahuatl *tle* and *inin*. There are no instances where the Nahuatl terms for close kin and the cardinal directions are replaced by their Spanish counterparts. There is not even one example of a Nahuatl inanimate noun being pluralized based on the Spanish model. On the contrary, all 111 items are of a type compatible with stage 2 although several may have come into Nahuatl in stage 3 (refer to Appendixes 1-4 for the discussion that follows).

The speaking parts draw most of the 111 loans from a small pool of older church items. The name or title *Dios* is by far the most frequent. It alone accounts for fully 317 spoken occurrences in the seven plays' total of 784 occurrences (or some 40 percent of the total). *Dios* ranges from a low of 18.6 percent of the loan frequency in "The Three Kings" to highs of 55.8 percent in "The Sacrifice of Isaac" and 62.8 percent in "How to Live on Earth."[24] It is one of the oldest, with attested first appearances in 1548.[25] The five most frequently spoken loans—*Dios, ánima, misa, Jesucristo,* and *Lucifer*—account for 412 occurrences out of 784 (some 52.5 percent) and appear in Nahuatl documents no later than 1552. I judge 16 of the 20 most frequently used items to be primarily ecclesiastical. Those 16 come to 537 occurrences out of 784 (68 percent of the total), and all appear in various types of Nahuatl texts no later than the early seventeenth century.

The church bias is stronger yet when the more mundane loans are taken into account. By my reckoning there are approximately one hundred total occurrences of such items in the seven plays. These include terms for money (*peso[s]* and *tomin[es]*), measurements of time (*domingo* and *hora*), legal terms and posts (*juramento, justicia, juez, testamento, testigos, escribano,* and *escritura*), designations of rank and function (*alcalde, conde, marqués, rey[es],* and *emperador*), and Spanish-style objects (*puerta* and *mesa*). Fifty-four of those occurrences are in "The Merchant." In some cases this one play contains all, or almost all, of the most frequently used. "The Merchant" has sixteen out of seventeen total occurrences in the seven plays of *pesos* and ten out of thirteen occurrences of *tomín,* as well as all occurrences of *tomines* (6), *testamento* (5), *peso* (4), *escribano* (2), and *escritura* (2). The already strongly ecclesiastical tone of the other six plays would be intensified if this play were excluded.

Focusing on the spoken loans reduces drastically the number of names being bandied about. Traditional social mores discouraged the use of individuals' names in direct address. All eight occurrences of the name Isaac in "The Sacrifice of Isaac" are about him, not directed to him personally. Nonetheless there was no absolute prohibition either. Once, in the same play, the slavewoman Hagar speaks of Abraham to her son Ishmael. However, the other four instances are in direct address: God the Father repeats Abraham's name twice in rapid succession, and his angel later does the same. Evidently this was a standard attention-getting device. Perhaps it was also permissible in these circumstances because social superiors (and who could be higher in a Christian-conceived social hierarchy than God and His angels?) were addressing a social inferior.

In "The Three Kings," ten out of seventeen spoken occurrences of Herod's name are in direct address, nine times by the three kings or Herod's priests, the tenth by Herod himself (unique in all the plays). Herod never addresses Casper, Melchior, or Balthasar by name but only in exalted and respectful terms. From a Nahua perspective, this pattern marks Herod as a vile character lower in status than the visiting kings. Although not a precise time-delineating marker, this usage would be more typical—or perhaps it would be more accurate to say stronger and more prevalent—earlier in the colonial period rather than later.

Many dimensions of loan meanings cannot be fully examined here. One that merits some attention is the use of *Jesús* less as a name or title than as an exclamatory indication of strong emotion. Out of nine occurrence only two are shorthand for Jesus Christ: 1 of 1 occurrence in "The Merchant" and 1 of 4 occurrences in "The Life of Don Sebastián."[26] The other seven all convey some combination of astonishment, dread, and bewilderment: 1 of 1 occurrence in "Souls and Testamentary Executors," 2 of 2 occurrences in "Final Judgment," 1 of 1 in "How to Live on Earth," and 3 of 4 in "The Life of Don Sebastián" (see ff. 44r, 4v, 18v, and pp. 17, 21). It is repeated in rapid succession in "Final Judgment" ("Jesus! Jesus!") and almost the same in "The Life of Don Sebastián" ("Jesus, what are you saying, Jesus!"). This more idiomatic usage (from a Hispanic standpoint) would be expected by the seventeenth century but not earlier.

A few of the loans have no dates of first appearance or present other minor problems of placement. Nonetheless, given the sometimes unusual references, this has more to do with hit-or-miss usage in very specialized Nahuatl genres or my lack of access to a broader database. There are also no problems presented by unanalyzed borrowed strings of words like *obra de misericordia*. These are typical of colonial Nahuatl texts. There is one such item, however, that I do not ever expect to find in the general corpus. The Latin phrase *surgite mortui venite a judicium* in "Final Judgment" was meant to be a high-sounding if meaningless (to the average Nahua parishioner) jumble of sounds (see f. 6v; the Latin means "Arise, O dead, and come to judgment"). These very same words, carved in stone, are prominently displayed on one of the processional chapels in the courtyard of the Franciscan church complex of San Andrés Calpan, Puebla. The processional chapel was completed circa 1550. It forms part of a dramatic rendering of the Last Judgment. Christ sits on his throne and beneath him is this stirring Latin phrase which was publicly exposed over decades and centuries to the Nahua parishioners of San Andrés Calpan. However, there is no compelling reason why even the few local notaries (who eventually learned to write both Nahuatl and Spanish) would have learned it and written it down in their documents. The sculpted images accompanying the meaningless words conveyed the essential information quite effectively, and besides, if anyone were curious about their meaning the local priest would have offered explanations in Nahuatl or Spanish. Hence finding an attestation for this Latin passage in any Nahuatl document (even in San Andrés Calpan) borders, in practical terms, on the impossible (see photograph, page 40).

There is one notable calque in mixed Spanish/Nahuatl form. There are eight occurrences of the loanword *cuenta*, not with the more common meaning of "rosary bead(s), rosary," but with the sense of "accounting," as in "to give or make an accounting of [something to someone]." Seven of the eight occurrences use the Nahuatl verb *maca*, "to give," in a rather straightforward calque based on Spanish *dar cuenta de*, "to give an accounting of [something to someone]" (see "How to Live on Earth," f. 21v; "The Life of Don Sebastián," p. 19; and "Final Judgment," ff. 2r, 3r, 5r [twice], and 7r). The eighth uses Nahuatl *chihua* "to make" as part of the related Spanish idiom "to make an accounting of [something to someone]" (see "Final Judgment," f. 7r). They appear in "Final Judgment" (6), "How to Live on Earth" (1), and "The Life of Don Sebastián" (1).

This is one of the few fully attested anticipations of stage 3. Undeniable confirmation of its stage 2 authenticity appears in the so-called *Diario* of Chimalpahin, the greatest Nahua annalist of the colonial period. In his entry for Saturday, January 21, 1612, he goes on at length about a troublesome—and apparently troubled—priest, fray Jerónimo de Zárate. He ruminates a bit about the cleric's questionable activities, perhaps consoling himself somewhat with the thought that "ma çan icel yc quimomaquiliz cuenta in totecuiyo Dios" (he alone will have to give an accounting of it to our lord, God). A few lines later he adds that when Zárate dies, "yc cuenta quimomaquiliz" (he will have to give an accounting of it to him; Chimalpahin 1965, 2:103). Added support comes from the published Nahuatl translation of the life of Saint Anthony of Padua by fray Juan Bautista and Agustín de la Fuente (1605). Here *cuenta* appears once as part of the calque and then in the general sense of "accounting": "quimmacaz melahuac cuenta in Officiales) (he will give a true accounting [of it] to the [king's] officials) and "Xiccuilican, xiccelilican, cuenta inin tlacatl" (take and receive an accounting [of this matter] from this person; Bautista 1605, 49r).

The general tenor of the loans suggests a stage 2 origin for the plays. Nonetheless there are at least two borrowings that smack of early stage 3. During his fulminating at the priests in "The Three Kings," Herod twice uses *judiazos* and *chicharrones*. The former contains the derogatory augmentative suffix *-zo* and is correctly inflected for the masculine plural *-os*. The latter is correctly inflected for the plural *-es*. Spanish as the language of insult is well attested among Nahuatl speakers today so this usage per se is not in question (see Hill and Hill 1986, 118–20). However, I intuitively feel that on balance this may imply a greater knowledge of the subtleties of Spanish than perhaps even Chimalpahin or Agustín de la Fuente possessed at the beginning of the seventeenth century, and it may be more appropriately associated with the period around 1700.[27]

Whenever appropriate the loans are Nahuatlized in ways typical of the time. One of the most interesting examples is *pexotli*, which can be found in a nonspeaking portion of "Final Judgment" (f. 6r). A tiny group of very early Spanish loan nouns bear what has been called the Nahuatl "absolutive suffix." In this particular case, the absolutive suffix *-tli* is attached to Spanish *peso*, "weight; scales." This attests to its very early entry into Nahuatl as well as to the (usually) unmarked glottal stop present in every borrowed Spanish noun that ended in a vowel.[28] The presence of orthographic *x* for *s* is probably a clue to its actual pronunciation by Nahuatl speakers, who early on would have substituted the affricate [š] for the Spanish sibilant.[29]

Sociopolitical terms also provide some clues to dating. Lockhart has correctly stated that, with regard to "political organization and kinship" as well as to "social rank," circa 1650 "proves to be a watershed in the evolution of vocabulary and concepts" (1992, 117). For example, such traditional terms for town council officeholders as *teteuctin*, "lords," and *pipiltin*, "nobles," are nonexistent or rare in eighteenth-century documents (1992, 49). He has not seen *tlatoani*, "dynastic ruler," used in that sense after 1661 (1992, 132). Wherever there is occasion to use such terminology in the plays, there is a decided bias toward the pre-1650, rather than the post-1650, period. This again speaks to probable dates of composition and/or copying that center on the seventeenth century, in particular the first half.

The traditional Nahuatl high rhetoric called *huehuetlatolli*, especially evident in pieces like "The Sacrifice of Isaac" and "The Three Kings," is also much more common prior to 1650.[30] There is a very precious and revealing detail of the *huehuetlatolli* in these plays that throws light on the entire group of plays and suggests some concrete, if tentative, conclusions about their origins.

The largest collection of explicitly prehispanic-style *huehuetlatolli* is contained in what is known today as book 6 of the twelve-book *Florentine Codex*. The entire work began in the late 1540s and went through various revisions and versions over the next thirty years. The editor of record was fray Bernardino de Sahagún. During the sixteenth century, the expertise in Nahuatl of this prominent Franciscan was equaled or surpassed only by a fellow Franciscan, fray Alonso de Molina, who had learned it as a small child and had native-speaker fluency. Notwithstanding Molina's preeminence in the language of everyday life, the Franciscan *nahuatlato* fray Jerónimo de Mendieta would aver that in "los secretos y antigüedades de la lengua ha alcanzado más que él ni otro ninguno" (the subtleties and ancient usages of the language [Sahagún] has achieved more than [Molina] or anyone else).[31] Sahagún directed a large and able group of Nahua collaborators, some his former students literate in Nahuatl, Spanish, and Latin.[32]

Another collection of *huehuetlatolli* pertains to the circle of the greatest colonial grammarian of Nahuatl, the Jesuit *nahuatlato* Father Horacio Carochi. The text is known today as the *Bancroft Dialogues*. They can be appreciated in a critical edition by Frances Karttunen and James Lockhart (1987). Two sections of those dialogues (one rather lengthy) closely parallel parts of chapter 10 of book 6 of the *Florentine Codex*. These borrowings establish beyond reasonable doubt that the mid-seventeenth-century Jesuit had access to the precious fruits of earlier Franciscan and Nahua scholarship (Karttunen and Lockhart 1987, 11–13).[33] No less certain is a similar connection between two sections of "The Three Kings" and the same chapter 10 of book 6 of the *Florentine Codex*.[34] Intriguingly, both the *Bancroft Dialogues* and "The Three Kings" borrow from the same pages (Sahagún 1950–1982, 6:47–49). The chapter is devoted to the installation of a new ruler and lamentations on the death of the old one. The three texts are noticeably close at times, but they are not identical. Compare the following excerpts from Sahagún's work and the play:

auh in aoc nane, in aoc tate in cujtlapilli, in atlapalli, auh in aoc ixe, in oc nacace, in aoc iyollo in atl, in tepetl: in ma iuh nontica, in amo naoati, in amo tlatoa in ma iuhquj quechcotontica.
(And the vassals no longer possess a mother, no longer possess a father. And no longer doth the city have the able, the prudent. They are as if mute; they speak not; they talk not; they are as if beheaded.) (Sahagún 1950–1982, 6: 47)

auh canel aocmo nane aocmo taye in cuitlapilli in atlapalli Auh canel aocmo ixxe in aocmo nacaçe in iuhqui nontiticac in amo nahuati in amo tlatohua innniuhqui quechcotonticac.
(And truly the tail, the wing [i.e., the vassal] no longer has a mother, no longer has a father. And truly it no longer has eyes, it no longer has ears [i.e., it lacks prudence]. It is as if it stands mute. It does not speak, it does not talk. It is as if it stands beheaded.)[35]

In his prologue to the *Sermonario* of 1606, fray Juan Bautista wrote that he and Agustín de la Fuente had compiled a three-volume collection of plays, which they intended to publish. They had already published a collection of elegant *huehuetlatolli* in 1600 that was based on work from sixty years before. Bautista explicitly acknowledged that they drew from the works of many eminent Nahua and Franciscan writers including Sahagún. They included parts of Sahagún's sermons in their sermonary. Their entire trajectory speaks of reviewing an extensive corpus of the best and most varied older writings, and then copying and revising them in preparation for publication. The three volumes of plays are among several works that unfortunately never left the press.

Given the above, I tentatively conclude that most or even all of the plays in their present form came from the texts gathered for Bautista and de la Fuente's three unpublished volumes of Nahuatl plays. The Franciscan *nahuatlato* and his trilingual Nahua coauthor—like no one else before or since—had the motivation, opportunity, training, and support needed to collect such materials and work them up. The textual ties to Sahagún in "The Three Kings" and the Franciscan jurisdiction where "The Merchant" was copied reinforce my supposition. The less-author-specific clues mentioned above point to circa 1600 (when Bautista and de la Fuente were active) as a time of likely copying and rearranging. Since I judge that some or all of the plays passed through—rather than originated at—their hands, there is the strong possibility that many arose in some fashion before, perhaps even well before, 1600.[36]

Caution is necessary in attribution, given the types of clues found in the texts themselves. It is further required since we can only appreciate these writings in their now-extant forms; most, perhaps all, can with varying justification be said to be later copies of older originals. The reader should thus regard the following as suggestions rather than ironclad conclusions. I consider "The Sacrifice of Isaac," "Souls and Testamentary Executors," "The Three Kings," and "The Merchant" in their currently known colonial versions as the most probable yields of the Bautista and de la Fuente collaboration. I deem "Final Judgment" and "How to Live on Earth" to be less certain products of their hands. I judge "The Life of Don Sebastián" to be the least certain, and in fact it may be a genuine product of the late seventeenth century. In any case, now that the plays are in more reliable transcriptions and their originals all located, a new round of scholarly analysis can more precisely verify or disprove these tentative assertions.

Life in the *Altepetl*: The Setting of "The Merchant"

Other contributors to this volume comment far more knowledgeably than I could on some of the otherwordly aspects of the dramas. I will discuss some of their more mundane features with a special focus on "The Merchant." Here as elsewhere the emphasis is on drawing out characteristics of the plays that may not be obvious to the general reader.

The arena in which the plays' Nahua characters, Christian supernaturals, and biblical figures mingle and interact is the *altepetl*. The term is a quasi-compound derived from the metaphorical doublet *(in) atl (in) tepetl* (the water, the hill), which refers to two essentials of community life. Postcolonial scholars have variously rendered it as tribe, village, empire, city, city-state, people, settlement, nation, and kingdom. My own preferences run to characterizing it most often as an ethnic city-state of greatly varying size.[37] This sociopolitical entity and its subdivisions are the overwhelming referent in the notarial corpus when Nahua scribes referred to unit identity. Its infrequent appearance in the dramas belies its importance. It is only within the framework of *altepetl* roles and expectations that the characters are most fully understood.[38]

A prime example is provided by the use of the term *tlatoani* (plural *tlatoque*), the traditional dynastic ruler of the altepetl and one of its defining features. The main thrust has to do with someone in charge who says things, that is, "Speaker" rather than "speaker," hence "one who issues commands, who gives orders," hence "ruler, governor." Since colonial times it has often been translated *rey*, "king." Indeed in "The Three Kings," Nahuatl *tlatoque* is paired a number of times with the Spanish loanword *reyes*, "kings."[39] Here the more neutral designation "ruler" has been chosen to avoid too easily casting Nahua *tlatoque* into the role of exotic "Indian kings." The word is present in all the plays. It is used in several ways typical of the 1540–1650, or stage 2, period: as a title of the ruler of an *altepetl* (Abraham), as one of the most frequently used epithets of the Christian deity (God), and in the more general sense of an important person who is not a ruler or even of noble birth (the avaricious merchant).

The *tlatoani* stood in a distinctly non-European relationship to the *altepetl*. Named subunits called *tlaxilacalli* (etymology uncertain) or *calpolli*, "big house," were the building blocks of the late prehispanic and colonial *altepetl*. They stood in relationship to each other in accordance with what Lockhart has termed a cellular or modular type of organization. *Altepetl* were created by the "aggregation of parts that remain[ed] relatively separate and self-contained, brought together by their common function and similarity, their place in some numerical or symmetrical arrangement, their rotational order, or all three" (Lockhart 1992, 436; brackets mine). He adds that this contrasts with the more urban-centered and nucleated Spanish municipality, which "stretched from a dominant center in the city to subordinate parts in the country" (1999, 100).

It is not surprising that Spaniards considered the area encompassing the residence of the current *tlatoani*—the central marketplace, nearby miscellaneous clusters of dwellings lying in distinct *tlaxilacalli*, and the main church (often the former site of the temple dedicated to the *altepetl*'s patron deity in prehispanic times)—as a *cabecera* (head town) and outlying *tlaxilacalli* or parts thereof as *sujetos* (dependencies; subject settlements). From their perspective, the early colonial *tlatoani* and his successor, the *gobernador* ("governor," or head of the local Spanish-style town council), was or should be in command of this so-called *cabecera* and its supposedly subordinate parts. However, from the Nahua perspective (at least for quite some time), this alleged urban center had no special status or name. *Tlatoque* and their later colonial counterparts were first and foremost based in their various *tlaxilacalli* and represented them. Ideally the highest-ranking members of these subunits rotated the post of *tlatoani*/governor according to some fixed order.

None of this is obvious in any of the plays, even in "The Merchant," which is the most naturalistic drama and the one on which I will focus below. "The Three Kings," with its emphatic use of late prehispanic forms of speech and social terminology, quite unselfconsciously pairs Nahuatl *tlatoque* with Spanish *reyes* (see above). This pairing may mislead the unwary reader. However, I take this usage to be no more or less expected than the many other shifting functional equivalencies that are rife within the extant Nahuatl and Spanish corpus when either party talked about the other. Each side long operated within its own conceptual framework and assumed that the other thought as it did (Lockhart [1992, 445] calls this process Double Mistaken Identity; for a current restatement of his position, see also 1999, 98–119). When communicating across cultural/linguistic borders, the tendency was to strive for pithy analogues rather than unwieldy longwinded definitions that took into account every conceivable similarity and difference. Both the Nahua and Spanish personages in question had power and authority over others, played vital roles in group unity and identity, and in other ways were essential parts of early modern Nahua and Spanish society.

The inhabitants and routines of the colonial *altepetl* are most fully represented by "The Merchant." In order of appearance, the cast comprises an unidentified speaker giving the prologue, Merchant, Old Man and Old Woman (an elderly couple), Young Woman, two sick people, Lowly Servant, Mature Man (married), Lord, an unidentified group of servants, Mother (accompanied now or later by nonspeaking children), Notary, Alcalde, Constable, Priest, Doctor, Sick Man (Merchant in his final agonies), Nobleman, several demons, the Merchant/Sick Man's wife, Guardian Angel, and two noblemen. Here we can see some of the rich complexity of Nahua society: the old and the young, those of varying degrees of wealth and poverty, men and women, nobles and commoners, people who are single or widowed or married, employers and employees, crucial *altepetl* officials, the healthy and the sick, members of various occupations (although farm folk and petty craftspeople are mostly implied), and even the presence of non-Nahuas, such as Priest. If one subtracts the obligatory opening speech, three quarters of the play passes in selected worldly pursuits before the first supernatural being makes his appearance. Customary activities include bargaining, borrowing and lending money, engaging the services of municipal officials, creating documents, and so on. The only comparable piece is "Souls and Testamentary Executors."

Lockhart suggests that these two dramas imply a subgenre (1992, 597n.120). There is a definite tilt in these two instances toward the confessionals' detailed presentations of the seventh commandment against stealing than toward the oftentimes more abstract offerings found in doctrinals and sermonaries.

Given a lingering popular conception that Spaniards overwhelmed and controlled passive native subjects, it is noteworthy that the few non-Nahuas in the plays have ineffectual powers of persuasion and nothing more. The priest in "The Merchant" is completely unsuccessful when he tries to persuade Merchant to show mercy to Mother and her two children, or when he pleads with Merchant's metamorphosed self, Sick Man, to make the true confession that will spare him the torments of hell. The cleric in "Final Judgment" is shocked by Lucía's confession but can do nothing beyond registering shock and horror. The priest in "Souls and Testamentary Executors" enjoys no real success with the spouse of don Pedro, for she is already observing all necessary Nahua and Christian protocols. In short, these church-sponsored dramas seem to undercut the moral stature of priests by denying them an authority they allegedly possessed.

Nahua *altepetl* often enjoyed considerable autonomy, survived in admirable fashion catastrophic imported epidemics that took off perhaps 95 percent of their numbers by the beginning of the seventeenth century, and seemingly always bedeviled their official spiritual advisers with their non-Christian beliefs and behaviors.[40] Among many pertinent colonial comments is the following marginal note (or lamentation?) from the Bautista and de la Fuente sermonary of 1606: *"La facilidad con que los naturales se juntan con Mestizos, y Españoles para contra su ministro, y padre"* (the ease with which the natives join with mestizos and Spaniards against their minister and priest; Bautista 1606, 617). Earlier marginalia drive home the point that "base and vile people" provoke damaging testimony against priests, and later marginalia almost wistfully enjoin Nahua parishioners to follow the lead of Saint Francis by loving and revering their spiritual fathers (Bautista 1606, 49, 616; cited in Sell 1993, 225n.219, 226n.225, respectively). Bautista's dismal view of Nahua treatment of the clergy is echoed decades later by the secular cleric (and mestizo) don Bartolomé de Alva [Ixtlilxochitl] in his confessional manual of 1634. Regarding taking the name of God in vain, Alva asks: "Perhaps some bad Spanish Christian paid you so that you would take an oath against a priest or some other honorable person, or someone who is a representative of the devil—through and because of you—wants to dishonor him, just taking his revenge and anger out on him?" (Sell and Schwaller 1999, 91–93).

The plays make no mention of one profound reality of early modern Nahua life: the nonclerical and nonroyal "mestizos and Spaniards" who evidently formed a considerable part of the "base and vile people" who set Nahuas against God's representatives on earth. The absence of ethnic, racial, or national diversity is perhaps the single most serious omission in the plays. The human landscape of Nahua Mexico has been reduced to a purist version of Nahua-only communities served by presumably Spanish priests. The contradiction between dramatized impression and recorded fact is stark in "The Merchant." The brief remarks in Nahuatl at the beginning of this play place it in Tollantzinco in 1687. Ten years later, the noted Franciscan chronicler fray Agustín de Vetancurt would write that Tollantzinco, ministered to by his order, contained more than fifteen hundred natives and more than six hundred Spaniards and mestizos (Vetancurt 1982,

63). Furthermore, the natives were not purely Nahuas: Tollantzinco was also home to Otomis, a people of distinct culture and language who were marginalized by the Nahuas in central Mexico (Lockhart 1991, 26–27). Interaction was intense among people of differing backgrounds and status in provincial capitals like Tollantzinco and the kinds of places where the plays would have been performed.

Operating within an increasingly variegated colonial context that is scarcely mentioned in the play, the chief protagonist of "The Merchant" is easy enough to recognize from the Nahuatl notarial record. Rebecca Horn's work provides a salient example close to 1630 when the play may have been copied or composed. (The following is drawn from Horn 1998, 75–76; Horn 1997b, 115, 135, 206; and from the testament of Juan Fabián that she used and that can be found in transcription and translation in Anderson et al. 1976, 58–63). Juan Fabián lived in Coyoacan, a large altepetl in the Valley of Mexico southwest of Mexico City. He made his testament in 1617. This well-to-do Nahua commoner traded in the native fruit called *zapotl* ("zapote"), probably grown on the orchard he possessed. He also owned a substantial amount of other land, at least one parcel of which had been purchased. He employed local Nahuas including carpenters. He had a horse, several mules, and sacks and pack gear. He very actively lent money to, and borrowed money from, both Nahuas and Spaniards. Neither this real-life example of a Nahua merchant nor Merchant from the play was overwhelmed by commerce, monetary dealings, or the market economy.

Many routine economic activities largely escape Nahuatl documentation.[41] Even when they do appear, we often see only a part of the process. The initial contracting of obligations like debts is infrequent in the extant record.[42] Mention of such financial dealings is most recurrent in testaments, because the obligations remained outstanding and needed to be satisfied by heirs or testamentary executors. Yet even while one often finds details about amounts, names, and circumstances,[43] there are rarely any particulars regarding fixed schedules of payment of specific amounts of principal and interest. Therefore, a discussion of the details of Merchant's financial dealings is in order before proceeding to a consideration of how typical or atypical the general circumstances were, as well as whether they contain welcome clues to how such financial transactions were structured. For ease of presentation, I will follow the order in which they appear in the play.

Merchant's first transaction involves Old Man and Old Woman. They need ten pesos so their son, now in police custody, will not be bound over to a textile manufacturing shop. Merchant charges ten pesos at 50 percent interest, that is, four *tomines* for each peso lent (since each peso equals eight *tomines*). They are to pay within fifteen days. If they fail to meet the two-week deadline, they are to pay twenty pesos, that is, interest plus penalty will equal 100 percent of the principal. When the fifteen days have passed, Merchant sends an underling to collect the money. Lowly Servant threatens them with jail or seizure of their property if they do not immediately make payment. Evidently they were successful in meeting the deadline for they hand Lowly Servant the full amount due.

Young Woman asks for a loan of twenty pesos so she can take care of her ailing parents, and she offers some personal items as collateral. She promises to make restitution in twenty days. She makes no mention of paying interest. Merchant cackles that he is not about the business of lending money to a crying pretty woman like herself but rather seeks an increase of his wealth. He proposes as absolute conditions that she pay 50 percent interest, that is, the twenty pesos principal plus ten pesos in interest, and that he might knock a little off the interest if she services him sexually. She indignantly refuses.

The two sick people who beg alms of Merchant mention no specific amounts before they are run off by his servants. Given the didactic character of the play, I would guess that a token amount such as a *tomín* or two was implied. This particular transaction is one of the instances that are most obviously gauges of the Merchant's propensity for shortchanging the spiritual side of his transactions.

Mature Man approaches Merchant with a request. He is going to Guatemala to get his spouse. He asks Merchant to guard one thousand pesos for him until his return. Four months pass. Mature Man reappears and asks for his money back. Merchant greets him politely enough but claims to know nothing about the entrusted amount. Mature Man asks him to take an oath on a cross and affirm that he does not, indeed, have the money. Merchant complies by laying his hand on the cross, swearing a false oath, and taking the name of God in vain. The episode ends with Merchant's servants driving Mature Man away with severe blows. This is another egregious instance of Merchant shortchanging himself spiritually.

Merchant deals quite differently with Lord. This high nobleman requests a loan of four thousand pesos for one month. Merchant agrees immediately, merely adding that Lord will need to pay four hundred pesos, that is, ten percent interest, on the principal. Lord agrees.

The last episode is the most complicated. Mother asks Merchant to give her the testament of her deceased husband (perhaps held in trust or against some incurred debt) so that she and her two children can lay claim to his estate. Merchant denies he has such a document. He claims that he bought the land and fields she mentions from her spouse, and that he knows nothing of any money and gems. He then insultingly speculates that perhaps she herself dissipated the items in question, or that her late husband did not make a testament, or that she and some unnamed companion (perhaps an illicit lover?) squandered the property. He calls her a drunk, urges her to sleep it off, and peremptorily bids her farewell. She once again appeals to his compassion only to be rudely rebuffed for a second time. He then summons Notary to create a false document (the testament mentioned below?), backdated three years, that supports his theft. Notary asks to be paid for his counterfeit paper trail and Merchant promises recompense.

Meanwhile, Mother appeals to Alcalde, who sends Constable to bring Merchant to him. Merchant comes before this representative of the local *cabildo*, once more lays his hand on a cross, swears an even stronger false oath, inviting the devil to take him if he lies, and again takes the name of God in vain. Notary produces the sham document, which alleges that Merchant paid one thousand pesos for the husband's house and fields. He further substantiates Merchant's lies by asserting that he witnessed both the money changing hands and the making of the dead man's testament. Alcalde dismisses Mother's claims.

Priest makes a final effort at moral persuasion but Merchant is adamant. This series of compounded transgressions against God and man evidently shifts the balance of Merchant's spiritual account too far into debt. Merchant becomes Sick Man, who in short order falls deathly ill. His ill-gotten earthly goods now do him no good. Just before he is strangled by demons, the once arrogant merchant calls in two noblemen to make his testament and take charge of distributing his spiritually worthless wealth. God's justice has been served.

Of this wealth of details concerning typical behaviors and attitudes, I will mention only a few. Merchant twice swears a false oath on the cross, taking the Lord's name in vain. The second time he adds for effect that if he is lying let it be God's will "that the devil take me." This clearly violates the second commandment: "HAVE you sometime falsely sworn the honored name of God? You did it on a cross? You took an oath, by means of swearing, and you verified what you know is not true?" (Sell and Schwaller 1999, 91).[44] Taking oaths on the cross was widespread although not always recorded. In a civil suit in Tlaxcala in 1568, a group of witnesses were required to swear in the name of God and Saint Mary, with their right hands on the cross, which they had kissed, that they would answer truthfully. If they lied, the devil would punish them; if they told the truth, God would have mercy on them (Sullivan 1987, 125). In a Tlaxcalan criminal case of 1565, several witnesses were deposed in similar fashion, although there was no mention of diabolical punishment or divine mercy (Sullivan 1987, 308–9, 310–11, 314–15).

Alcalde hears Mother's complaint against Merchant. Alcaldes ranked higher than *regidores* (city councilmen) in colonial Nahua municipal government, just the opposite of what was true in Spanish *cabildos* (Lockhart 1992, 36–37). They were *cabildo* members, judges, and high-ranking members of their *altepetl*. Alcalde's ultimate collusion with Merchant's nefarious schemes, even if unwitting, is perhaps already suggested by the good relations enjoyed between Merchant and Lord. I find no hint that Merchant is anything more than a very wealthy commoner who has successfully parlayed his financial success into something approaching equality with the local high-born.

Other sorts of incidents would have little reason to appear in the Nahuatl notarial record. Merchant treats Old Man and Old Woman with active disdain when they appeal to him in their time of great need. This goes against the fifth commandment: "Did you honor your mother and your father, your elder brothers, the elderly men and women who were born first?" (Sell and Schwaller 1999, 101). More specifically, dutiful Nahua Christians were instructed: "Did you honor elderly men and elderly women? Or did you hold them in no regard? Did their miseries not inspire compassion in you? Did you not help them?" (Molina 1984, 30r).[45] This closely accorded with traditional Nahua notions concerning respect for the elderly as recorded in a collection of traditional *huehuetlatolli*. A young person of high station who is traveling is given instructions on how to properly greet commoners of advanced age. An old man is to be greeted with "Nottatzine nocoltzine, notlatzine" (O my father, O my grandfather, O my uncle) and an old woman with "Nonantzine, nocitzine" (O my mother, O my grandmother), to be followed by "ma ihuiyan ma icemel xommohuicatiuh, ma cana tommohuetziti" (May you be going along calmly and happily, may you not fall down somewhere; Bautista 1600b, 51v–52r).

A thread of physical violence runs through the plays. "The Merchant" contains some of the more explicit scenes. Merchant's servants run off the two sick people.

Later they run off Mature Man, "severely beating him." Near the end of the play, one of the demons strangles Merchant/Sick Man to death. Herod might be physically threatening the Jewish priests when he drives them away in "The Three Kings." Aside from the obvious close call in "The Sacrifice of Isaac," there is a threat of implied violence when Second Nobleman speaks of running off Hagar and Ishmael. Near the end of "Souls and Testamentary Executors," there is possible torture by the demons of the condemned. Don Sebastián murders his wife in "The Life of Don Sebastián." Woman walks along berating her son, Little Child, and slapping his face in "How to Live on Earth." Little Child speaks of seizing her by the hair. While in the forest, Third Youth speaks of beating and slapping his parents and seizing them by the neck. He is apparently killed by a fierce beast while his companions sleep. Death "kills" Lorenzo and his wife by shooting arrows. At the end of the play, Christ tells the demons to take Condemned One to the fiery cavern where he is to be hung, beaten, and broken to bits. Lucía in "Final Judgment" suffers at the end from her fiery apparel. Shortly thereafter, stage directions twice indicate that she is to be beaten by demons as they drive her into hell.

Familial-, gender-, and age-based violence is to some extent addressed in the questions standard in confessional manuals. Under the fourth commandment, to honor your father and your mother, are the queries: "Did you repeatedly beat them when you were drunk? Did you slap them in the face? Do you repeatedly kick them? . . . Perhaps you pulled out their facial hair or grabbed them by their hair as you are wont to do?" (Sell and Schwaller 1999, 101). Spouses were to be properly treated under the same commandment (Molina 1984, 29v). Physical abuse directed against the young was placed within other contexts such as drunkenness and the failure to treat one's family properly. When a drunkard comes home in a rage, "he beats his wife and children, kicking and kicking them, throwing earth at them" (Sell and Schwaller 1999, 121). This is apart from the equation made between abortion and murder in the fifth commandment (Molina 1984, 31v; Sell and Schwaller 1999, 103). Less routine types of violence get some play in the Nahuatl notarial record. There are several such incidences in the largest single collection of colonial Nahuatl testaments. These documents were generated in the *altepetl* of Culhuacan and almost all are from the years 1579–1589. One was an attack on a peace officer and another an interethnic assault, a black man who gravely wounded a Nahua (Cline and León-Portilla 1984, 136–37, 220–21).[46]

Old Man and Old Woman need their loan so they can free their son from what is evidently a stint of forced labor in an *obraje* (textile manufacturing shop) to pay off debts or a serious crime. Old Woman later remarks with some urgency to Old Man that the same could happen to them if they do not repay the merchant on time. She had heard in the marketplace that another couple suffered this very fate. Their fear of *obrajes* was well founded. From a business angle, *obrajes* had "high start-up and operating costs, modest profits, and low prestige" (Horn 1997b, 219). Since the resulting low wages were not sufficient to attract enough free workers, forced laborers like slaves and prisoners were often employed. They were literally locked up inside these notorious establishments (see Horn 1997b, 218–20, for more details on the presence and operation of *obrajes* in Coyoacan). Conditions were so bad that a manual for confessors of 1600 advised dealing leniently with Nahuas who worked in *obrajes* and stole from their owners. This was one of the few situations where the need to make restitution under the seventh commandment was relaxed: "Y comoquiera que no pueden restituir pues son alli perpetuos deudores y esclauos, no tienen obligacion de restituyr" (But inasmuch as they cannot make restitution since there they are perpetual debtors and slaves, they are not obliged [by the church] to make restitution; Bautista 1600a, 14r, brackets mine).

Going into debt to satisfy judicial penalties and paying or working off the debt thus incurred were accepted practices. There are two typical examples from the above-mentioned testaments of Culhuacan. In a testament of August 25, 1580, the widow María states that "my late second husband named Francisco Quauhtli and I borrowed a peso belonging to the ward heads so that we could leave jail when we were both imprisoned" (Cline and León-Portilla 1984, 79).[47] She then tries to make arrangements to discharge this financial burden. In the testament of February 12, 1581, of Luis Tlauhpotonqui, a *pochtecatl* or merchant like Juan Fabián mentioned previously, there again is a debt pending by "Miguel Huelilhuitl[:] . . . nine pesos. . . . And as to the three pesos which he paid, he just worked at our home to pay it. With this money he got out of jail, because he broke the head of Juan de San Miguel when he was *alguacil mayor*. And he is to pay this promptly" (Cline and León-Portilla 1984, 137).[47] It was also acceptable in some cases to compel people to work to pay off their transgressions. The Tlaxcalan *Actas* (town council minutes) for November 4, 1547, decree that a pay scale is being set for those Tlaxcalans "arrested for drunkenness and hired out as punishment" (Lockhart et al. 1986, 35).[48] The pay scale varies from two *tomines* to one peso per month depending on whether the labor is common or skilled, the work is in [Nahua] Tlaxcala or [Spanish] Puebla, and the employers are Tlaxcalans or Spaniards. Other instances of forced labor can be found in the *Actas* (Lockhart et al. 1986, 42 [item 54] and 45 [item 72]).

While the ten pesos requested by Old Man and Old Woman and the twenty pesos solicited by Young Woman are more or less within the upper range of similar dealings in Nahuatl testaments, the one thousand pesos entrusted to Merchant by Mature Man, the four thousand pesos loaned by Merchant to Lord, and the one thousand pesos supposedly paid to Mother's deceased husband by Merchant are unusually large sums. For comparison, I cite an instance recorded in the Tlaxcalan *Actas*. The minutes for May 1, 1562, state that the *altepetl* of Tlaxcala is borrowing four hundred pesos from the *altepetl* of San Andrés Calpan (located in the present-day state of Puebla). Somewhat in the fashion of Young Woman's initial proposal, they give no interest rate but pledge *altepetl* assets against the debt and promise to pay it back in ten months (Lockhart et al. 1986, 118–19). This is in response to ongoing financial difficulties and represents one of the largest strictly monetary sums in the twenty-year run of these town council minutes. An even larger sum is mentioned on December 18, 1553. The *altepetl* has formed a company with Juan Ruiz, "a Spaniard," and, as part of the deal, the *altepetl* has bought thirty oxen, the cost so far coming to about eight hundred pesos (Lockhart et al. 1986, 90).[49] Horses and mules, high-value commodities in native communities, are assigned values from five to forty pesos (Cline and León-Portilla 1984, 105, 137, 155, 189, 275; Anderson et al. 1976, 60–63).

Other cash amounts mentioned in wills tend to be small, frequently measured in *tomines* rather than pesos. A debt of only four pesos caused considerable distress for one Joaquín Matlalacan of Culhuacan, who in his 1585 testament charges his executors with recovering the sum from his debtor, Gerónimo de San Mateo Tlalxopan: "Let the executors ask him for them in order that masses be said for me; many times I asked him for them, but he almost killed me over them" (Cline and León-Portilla 1984, 237). In Tollantzinco in 1582, the local church needed a bell, so the *altepetl* obtained a loan of one hundred pesos from a local Spaniard. After two and a half years, only half of the debt had been paid back. The Spanish creditor then took vigorous legal action. Part of the town's *cabildo* ended up in jail. All this over fifty pesos! (Lockhart 1991, 28–29). These amounts pale in comparison to the one thousand and four thousand pesos mentioned in the play. This strongly suggests that the amounts were exaggerated in order to increase their dramatic and didactic impact.

The one real surprise in the entire play is the emphasis on moneylending and the details concerning schedules of payment of principal and specified interest. Mention of usury in the ecclesiastical Nahuatl corpus is typically brief compared to the relatively copious amounts of ink spent on drunkenness and idolatry.[50] In the rather extensive section devoted to the seventh commandment against stealing in fray Alonso de Molina's confessional manual of 1569, almost lost among folio after folio of detailed questioning is the following: "Did you sometime loan at interest, did you perhaps lend things, so that you would be given [back] much more?" (Molina 1984, 41r).[51] Molina's book of Christian doctrine includes under the seventh commandment an equally brief mention of merchants who are moneylenders (Molina 1578, 37r).[52] Other references are usually just as brief.[53]

Usury receives more attention in the two-volume handbook on confession prepared by fray Juan Bautista and Agustín de la Fuente. In this 1600 imprint they write:

¶ En muchas partes desta nueua España, se vsan logros, prestando vna persona a otro vn peso, y rescibiendo despues dos, o poco menos y finalmente siempre mas de lo principal que se presta, ora sea en dineros, ora Mayz, o en otras semillas. Y muy pocos se acusan deste peccado, y asi sera bien que los predicadores de quando en quando prediquen contra el y los confessores pregunten a los Mercaderes o Indios ricos, si han dado a logro: para mandarles restituyr lo que asi vuieren lleuado. Ay proprio vocablo de logro, que es, tetech tlaixtlapanaliztli, tetech tlamieccaquixtiliztli, y para dezir diste a logro? Cuix tetech otitlaixtlapan, cuix [te]tech otitlamieccaquixti?

In many parts of this New Spain money is lent at interest, one person lending another one peso and afterwards receiving two or a little less, but in any case always more than the principal lent, whether it be in money or maize or other seeds. And very few confess to this sin, and so it would be good if once in a while preachers preached against it and the confessors question the merchants or rich Indians as to whether they have lent at interest with the aim of ordering them to make restitution of what they would have made. There is appropriate terminology for lending at interest which is tetech tlaixtlapanaliztli, tetech tlamieccaquixtiliztli. And in order to say "Did you lend money at interest?" [one says] "Cuix tetech otitlaixtlapan? Cuix [te]tech otitlamieccaquixti?" (Bautista 1600a, 15r–v; all brackets mine)

In 1713 the Augustinian fray Manuel Pérez commented on usury in his *Farol Indiano*, a technical religious manual aimed at helping priests minister to Nahuas. In his view, although in general confessional inquiry about usury was best avoided so as not to teach bad behaviors, Nahuas of Mexico City did lend money at interest with the understanding that "mientras dura el no bolver the principal, esta el deudor dando cada semana vn tomin al acreedor" (as long as the principal has not been repaid the debtor gives a tomin each week to the creditor; Pérez 1713, 187). He adds that he has heard of such practices both in confession and out of it from both creditors and debtors. Fifty years later appeared the combination grammar–dictionary–confessional manual (1765) of Bachiller Don Jerónimo Tomás de Aquino Cortés y Zedeño. This secular cleric in the bishopric of Guadalajara asks if the confessee has lent three *reales* in order to receive four *reales* back (33 pecent interest), or lent four pesos in order to get four pesos and four *reales* back (12.5 percent interest). He next asks if the confessee has made loans in kind of such goods as maize, beans, and wheat, expecting to receive more back than he lent (Cortés y Zedeño 1967, 169–70).

These testimonies suffice to establish that moneylending at interest was practiced by Nahuas, at least to some extent, and hence there was some context for a didactic play in which it is a featured sin. Details of the practice—both in the play and in the statements cited above—vary considerably; the inconsistencies in Merchant's behavior may, thus, be compatible with native practice even while the size of some of the loans is highly exaggerated.

As in so much else, this play like the others ultimately offers very few surprises or unusual challenges to researchers already familiar with the colonial Nahuatl corpus in both its civil and ecclesiastical components. The texts are skewed to serving Christian didactic ends, distorting and/or illuminating in ways that are often predictable and expected. This should not detract from their intrinsic value to the interested reader. Here is early Nahua culture and language presented in a fairly lively fashion in a genre unique among Native American alphabetical texts.

Notes

1. Mesoamerica is a culture area comprising much of what is now modern Mexico and northern Central America.

2. I am thinking here of the Nahuatl censuses of the Morelos region. For a representative sample in transcription and translation with commentary, see Cline 1993.

3. Due to last-minute considerations of space, the second version of "How to Live on Earth" will appear in Volume 4.

4. This fundamental sociopolitical unit of Nahua life will be discussed in some detail below, but for now the reader should be aware that contemporary Spaniards often translated the term as *ciudad* (city) and *pueblo* (people, settlement).

5. I first became aware of these documents from Lockhart (1992, 50). The originals are in the Special Collections Department of the University of California at Los Angeles.

6. Some of the plays have additions/corrections/changes in a hand different from that of the main text, suggesting that they were still works in progress.

7. The observant reader will note that the earlier reference to a Tollantzinco notarial document written on *Wednesday*, November 3, and this reference to *Saturday*, November 15, both in 1687, do not jibe.

8. The most prominent would be Oaxtepec, Morelos. The Dominicans built a church complex there, which can still be appreciated today.

9. Imagine my surprise when I inspected the original several years ago at the Library of Congress and could find no date whatsoever! My chagrin was somewhat lessened upon discovering that my coeditor repeated in good faith the same error (see Burkhart 1996, 282 n. 8).

10. Inaccuracies can be extremely hardy. The same faulty dating continues to appear in recent scholarship.

11. I gratefully acknowledge a deep debt to Fernando Horcasitas, John H. Cornyn, and Byron McAfee. I began in some cases with digitized versions of their transcriptions, which speeded my initial progress and also helped me realize just how different the new transcriptions were. I also twice personally consulted the four texts housed in the Library of Congress (LC) and doublechecked them against our evolving transcriptions. None of this would have been possible without the help of Greg Spira, who also helped with the first drafts of the LC transcriptions.

The four texts from the University of Michigan's Clements Library and the Academy of American Franciscan History were consulted via microfilm (exceptionally clear) and hard copy, respectively. Once digitized, all transcriptions were fully checked three (in some cases, four) times by Louise M. Burkhart and Barry D. Sell, over a period of two years. Inevitably there must be outright errors, but the editors have worked hard to minimize them.

12. At times it is a very subjective and frustrating exercise trying to settle on an individual scribe's intent (or lack thereof) regarding capitalization. The same is true of spacing.

13. Speaking only for myself, I generally follow the usages of fray Juan Bautista and Agustín de la Fuente. Their published work (1599–1607) anticipates modern norms in many particulars.

14. The second version of "How to Live on Earth" is the other play most like "Final Judgment" in this respect.

15. I am in general agreement with Lockhart (1991, 122–40) on the phoneticity of Nahuatl texts.

16. See "The Sacrifice of Isaac" for "oc cecppa" (28v) and "Oc çecppa" (30r). "Souls and Testamentary Executors" has even more examples: "oc çecppa" (39r, 40r, 51v), "ocecppa" (39v), and "oc cecppa" (43r). Although bound together with them, "The Three Kings" not only is written in a different hand but lacks this telltale marker.

17. A document from Xochimilco in 1572 uses *tç* for *tz*, apparently reflecting the influence of the renowned *nahuatlato* fray Bernardino de Sahagún who had been stationed there. The text can be found in Karttunen and Lockhart 1976, 94–96.

18. While I have conscientiously tried to verify this last statement, there may be one or two examples I have inadvertently missed. Given other considerations below, my first impression would be scribal error.

19. I have very occasionally encountered *hv*, which admittedly may contain nothing more than a stylized *u*. For some examples, see Karttunen and Lockhart 1976, 105.

20. Exceptions can be occasionally found such as in a 1572 document from Xochimilco (Karttunen and Lockhart 1976, 94–96). Sahagún's influence on the Nahua notary involved can be seen in the use of *ho* or *o* for prevocalic [hu] as in "mochihoaz" for *mochihuaz* or "nicpeoaltia*" for *nicpehualtia* (94). Even published clerical texts contain examples. Many can be found in Sahagún's own *Psalmodia christiana* (1583) and Arthur J. O. Anderson's critical edition of same (Sahagún 1993b).

21. The one exception can be found in "The Life of Don Sebastián" (p. 21): "Otlapopol*uis*" [italicization mine]. I regard this as simple scribal error. Here the Find command of my word processor (Word 5.1 for the Mac) was invaluable. I searched for and examined every single possible occurrence of *va/ua/hua, ve/ue/hue,* and *vi/ui/hui.*

22. The question of whether this orthographic shift implies changes in actual speech deserves a separate discussion.

23. For the sake of brevity I am oversimplifying. I urge the interested reader to consult Karltunen's and Lockhart's works directly.

24. From this point forward, unless otherwise indicated, "How to Live on Earth" refers to the first version, which forms the basis of the English translation included in this volume.

25. Those relatively few Nahuas living primarily among Spaniards at a very early time—the live-in Nahua pupils of the friars and full-time servants of Spaniards—surely recognized, and were using, *Dios* even before the appearance of alphabetical Nahuatl texts in the late 1530s.

26. See f. 52r and p. 13, respectively. My impression is that the use of *Jesús* gradually increases from the sixteenth to the eighteenth centuries.

27. For the circa 1700 period, I am thinking of the sorts of annals of which a representative sample can be found in Karttunen and Lockhart 1976, 114–15. Alternatively, Burkhart suggests (personal communication dated January 17, 2001) that perhaps this is an attempt to make Herod appear "ethnically Spanish in contrast to the Nahua (and so culturally superior) Magi." She adds that the author "may have imitated insults he heard Spaniards using, or asked a Spaniard to suggest appropriate terms." This may well be on the mark.

28. If written according to some colonial and current conventions, it would thus read (minus diacritics to indicate vowel length) *pexohtli*.

29. Regarding this and other very early loans with the absolutive suffix, consult Karttunen and Lockhart 1976, 21–22; Lockhart 1992, 295, 565n.82; and Sell 1993, 75–76. This and similar letter substitutions that correspond to actual Nahuatl speech provide another indication that native speakers wrote, copied, and rearranged the plays.

30. It would not be entirely correct to add that there were no late colonial attempts at writing down at least elements of early colonial *huehuetlatolli*. The well-read Jesuit *nahuatlato* Father Ignacio de Paredes admired it. He tried to use bits and pieces of it in the four publications that appeared under his name in 1758 and 1759.

31. Mendieta 1988, 558. Wayne Ruwet of the UCLA Library System first alerted me to this source. This translation differs somewhat from that in Sell 1993, 118.

32. See Sell 1993, 39–56, for the important role that literate Nahuas played in producing manuscripts and publications that rarely acknowledged their assistance.

33. Carochi also borrowed from the *Florentine Codex* in his grammar of 1645 (see Carochi 1983, 124v). The two parallel passages are compared side by side in Sell 1993, 45.

34. See Burkhart's notes in the translation of "Three Kings," ff. 17r–v, 19r–20r.

35. See ff. 17r–v and the facing translation of "The Three Kings" in this volume. Small changes were made here to fit the context.

36. The sermonary of 1606 by Bautista and de la Fuente included large chunks of Sahagún's 1548 sermonary (originally written in 1540). Their *huehuetlatolli* publication was based largely on the late 1540s work of the Franciscan *nahuatlato* fray Andrés de Olmos. In both cases, the team of Bautista and de la Fuente published texts that were first written fifty or more years before the publications appeared. Perhaps portions of some of the plays go back as far, although how to prove this remains a difficult task in the absence of relevant new primary sources.

37. For those not familiar with the specialized literature on the altepetl, a good beginning would be the relevant chapters and sections of Lockhart 1991, 1992, 1999.

38. The term itself appears once in "The Sacrifice of Isaac" and "The Merchant," twice in "The Life of Don Sebastián," and fifteen times (plus two unspoken) in "The Three Kings."

39. Every time *reyes* is used, it is paired with *tlatoque* (four times in spoken dialogue, three times in unspoken sections) and bears the Nahuatl pluralizing suffix *-me*. The Nahuatl term

always comes first. During the early colonial period, such a pair was probably interpreted by the average Nahua listener as *"tlatoque,* [what Spanish-speaking people would call] *reyes."*

40. The seemingly endless campaigns against idolatry, along with the manuscripts and books written to aid priests in those efforts, attest to the survival of non-Christian beliefs and practices. See Sell and Schwaller 1999 for a recent critical edition of one such work.

41. A point well made by Lockhart: "Since the routine of daily life consists of an almost infinite number of discrete small actions and strategies, its elements must have seemed individually too insignificant (as well as too obvious or presupposed) to deserve space on the written page. . . . Nahuatl writing is never merely discursive but always for a specific purpose; in mundane Nahuatl documentation, that purpose is generally to claim or protect rights or possessions that might be legally challenged. In the sphere of marketplace activity, the crafts, and the production, sale, and consumption of agricultural commodities, challenges apparently did not reach the level of legal action within the altepetl framework" (1992, 176).

42. Intent to borrow is mentioned in the Tlaxcalan *Actas* (*cabildo* minutes), to be discussed later.

43. This is true of Juan Fabián's testament (Anderson et al. 1976, 58–63) and that of another Nahua merchant, Luis Tlauhpotonqui (in transcription and translation in Cline and León-Portilla 1984, 134–43).

44. This is standard fare in confessional manuals directed toward Nahuas. For an earlier example, see Molina 1984, 25v.

45. The Nahuatl reads: "¶ Cuix otiquimmahuiztili yn veuetque, yn ilamatque: acaçomo tle ypan tiquimittac, acaçomo mitztlaocoltia, yn intlayhiyohuiliz, acaçomo tiquimpalehui?" The facing Spanish reads: "¶ Honraste y reuerenciaste a las personas ancianas: o dexaste de tenerles el deuido respecto, no teniendo compassiõ de sus miserias, dexandolos de ayudar?"

46. The third case is in Cline and León-Portilla (1984, 237) and is mentioned below.

47. By "ward heads," she literally means those in charge of the *tlaxilacalli,* or the "tlaxillacalleque" (Cline and León-Portilla 1984).

48. A transcription and translation of this portion of the minutes can be found in Anderson et al. 1976, 118–21.

49. Another large sum, 300 pesos for two chasubles, is the next item of business mentioned.

50. For the latter two topics, Bartolomé de Alva, 1634 (Sell and Schwaller 1999) is one example among many.

51. This is my translation of the Nahuatl. The Nahuatl and facing Spanish read: "¶ Cuix yca tetech titlayxtlapan, cuix noço ytla tictetlacuilti, ynic oc ye cenca miec timacoz?" / "¶ Diste alguna vez algo a logro, o prestaste alguna cosa, para que te la boluiessen con crecida ganancia?"

52. The main text is in Nahuatl with headings and indexes in Spanish. The Nahuatl reads: "Auh in ampuchteca, macamo tetech xitlaixtlapanacā, macamo tetech xitlamieccaquixtican."

53. For some examples, see Molina's small confessional manual of 1565, 15r; Bautista 1599, 32v; and Lorra Baquío 1634, 73r.

DEATH AND THE COLONIAL NAHUA

Louise M. Burkhart

In his study of death in sixteenth-century Spain, Carlos Eire writes: "[D]eath was the unique moment, common to all, when the church could make the ultimate claim over each individual and over society as a whole; it was arguably the consummate Catholic experience, the ultimate expression of a society's beliefs, and also the ultimate opportunity for shaping and controlling a society's behavior" (1995, 5). Pious Spaniards sought not only to live good lives but to die good deaths. They were in the latter endeavor aided by a plethora of guidebooks as well as such exemplary models as Philip II and Teresa de Ávila (Eire 1995). Preconquest Mexicans held very different beliefs about the dissolution of the self at death and the dispersal of its components, which included multiple animating essences. Becoming colonial and becoming Christian demanded considerable accommodations in the views and practices associated with death, including adjustments to the mass deaths brought about by Old World infectious diseases.

The Church's intrusion into the emotional experience of bereavement and the social realignment brought about by the loss of a family and community member can be seen as one strategy for "shaping and controlling" indigenous behavior in ways that furthered the hegemony of Spanish religious and legal institutions. Colonizing death helped to colonize the living as well, although, as with all colonial introductions, Nahuas manipulated the new ways of dying for their own purposes.

The plays "How to Live on Earth," "The Merchant," "Final Judgment," "The Life of Don Sebastián," and "Souls and Testamentary Executors" all focus on human moral behavior and its punishment or reward. These morality plays, with their graphic representations of the soul's fate, were intended to persuade Nahua audiences to accept and conform to Catholic moral teachings, principally by displaying the frightful posthumous consequences of disobedience. The five plays share a common—and bleak—moral vision, one of human frailty, demonic temptation, angelic despair, and sudden death. Demons bear some of the blame for humanity's dire state, but they, like Death, are subject to divine authority and are only doing their job. The human characters are responsible for their own fates. They repent, too late to save themselves but in time to warn others. The obligation to care for souls in purgatory is a recurring theme, as is the infernal fate of recalcitrant sinners. The five plays can be considered a subgenre of Nahuatl drama, and they may be a remnant of a much larger corpus of morality plays that circulated among colonial Nahua communities.

The purpose of this essay is to situate these five morality plays within a wider universe of discourse on death in the colonial Nahua setting, examining how Christian concepts of death and the afterlife were presented to and by Nahuas in other contexts. To gain some understanding of how Nahua audiences would have received and interpreted these dramas, it may be useful to examine what they were likely already to know about the topics they saw dramatized. Space does not permit a fuller explication of either the European or the indigenous cultural background, but I hope that the material I do present here will enhance readers' understanding of the five dramas.

Souls and Bodies

Teaching about death is one area in which we might expect the contradiction between indigenous monism and Christian dualism to be highlighted. At death, according to Christianity, the human person bifurcated itself into earthly body and immortal, immaterial soul, with the soul proceeding to an immaterial world beyond, its destination depending on the moral condition of the deceased. The sloughed-off earthly coil, despised in Catholic doctrine as an enemy of the soul for its carnal temptations, met its deserved fate in decay. While the fates of preconquest souls were not wholly divorced from the condition of their owners, as some deities chose certain people to join them in their afterworlds, notions of personal moral responsibility, with the promise of heavenly reward for good deeds and the threat of damnation for bad, were colonial introductions, difficult for priests to inculcate (Burkhart 1989). Souls did not belong to another world but were part of this world, manifested in visible, natural phenomena (Furst 1995).

The soul that most closely corresponded to the Christian notion was the *-yolia*, a life force housed in and closely associated with the heart *(yollotl)*, which was the seat of various cognitive as well as emotional processes (López Austin 1984, 1:207, 252–57).[1] The *-yolia* was considered a shadowy double of the person, though it could also manifest itself as a bird or a butterfly, as a stone, and as breath (Furst 1995). This was the one soul that retained an individual identity after death and also passed on to an afterworld, usually the shadowy *mictlan*, or underworld "place of the dead." Furst suggests that a pallid bird- or butterfly-shaped pattern that forms on the upper back of a corpse when the blood settles into the tissues was seen as a physical manifestation of the *-yolia* leaving the body (1995, 40–41). But the *-yolia* did not necessarily depart immediately or completely. In burials it was represented by a stone that was interred with the body or remains and that lent animating force to the bones (Furst 1995, 54, 59–61).

Friars introduced their own concept of the soul (Spanish *ánima*, Latin *anima*) by linking their word with *-yolia;* in colonial Nahuatl texts, the terms are used interchangeably and are often paired in a diphrase. While doctrinal texts pay much attention to the moral condition and fate of these essences, delineations of their precise nature and origin are lacking, allowing Nahuas to perpetuate their own beliefs and simply adopt *ánima* as a synonym for *-yolia*. In the texts quoted in this paper, I translate *-yolia* as "spirit" and *ánima* as "soul."

In the dramas, souls in the form of human actors are seen to leave their bodies, walk about, and talk, carrying on the deceased's identity and relationship to the living (speaking, for example, of "my wife" or "my relatives"). The souls of Lorenzo and his wife in "How to Live on Earth" are played by children; the actors playing the souls of several of the corrupt characters are to wear black clothing and/or makeup. It is unlikely that preconquest Nahuas thought of their *-yolia* in quite this way, but beliefs that the *-yolia* retained an individual identity and could appear as a double of the body provided precedents for these portrayals. Immorality, if not explicitly linked with the color black, was associated with dirtiness and bad odors, which the smell of the explosives used in the dramas might invoke. It is possible that Nahuas dressed the children playing the good souls as angels, which fit the *-yolia*'s identification as a bird. And these dramatized souls certainly appear as concrete beings manifested in this world, not as part of any ethereal beyond.

Nahuatl also lacked any term corresponding precisely to "body" (Spanish *cuerpo*, Latin *corpus*). The term usually used in colonial texts is *-nacayo*, or a person's *nacatl*, "meat or flesh," which is what I translate as "body" in the texts quoted below. This term properly referred to the soft tissues of the body, exclusive of the bones. These were the parts that decayed into the earth after death (or were burned away in cremation), leaving the bones, which retained something of the individual's vital forces (López Austin 1984, 1:176–77). The diphrase *in -tlallo in -zoquiyo*, "(one's) earth, (one's) mud," that appears in the dramas can substitute for *-nacayo*; it also suggests putrescible flesh rather than enduring bone. Thus, whereas European Christians considered the body a unit, Nahuas may have continued to make a meaningful distinction between soft tissue and bone. The former returned to the earth, the latter remained.

Bones figure in two of the plays. "How to Live on Earth" makes several references to the "bones and tibias" of the dead, which, for Nahuas, may serve not only as reminders of dead forebears but as manifestations of their ongoing essence. In "The Life of Don Sebastián," the character Death (Miquiztli) plunks the skulls of the dissolute nobleman's parents onto the table before him, a memento mori that was also a confrontation with parental authority. Death appears as a character also in "How to Live on Earth" and "Final Judgment." Probably costumed to look like a skeleton (Lucifer addresses him as "bones" in "The Life of Don Sebastián"), he too embodies the enduring life force of bones.[2] As Christ's constable, Death is a positive—not a fearsome—character in the plays, consistent with a distinction between fleshly decay and osseous vitality. Ideas about bones retaining a vital essence and having regenerative power might have informed native interpretations of the resurrection of the dead, enacted in "Final Judgment."

Preconquest Nahuas associated soul loss not with the *-yolia* but with the *tonalli*, an animating essence located in the head and associated with the sun's heat (López Austin 1984, 1:243–47). Even so, this idea that a soul could leave and return to the body was a precedent for the near-death experiences that colonial Nahuas occasionally reported, in which their spirit temporarily departed into the kind of afterworld presented to them in Christian preaching and dramas. Friars, seeing these reports as evidence of their own success, inscribed some of them in their chronicles. The scenarios vary: Mary, saints, friars coming to console the dying person (Mendieta 1980, 459-60; Dávila Padilla 1955, 146); a quick trip to hell, then to heaven, with instructions to confess in order to come there (Motolinia 1979, 95); black creatures dragging a young man off to a dark place of torments until he calls on Mary for help (Motolinia 1979, 95-96); demons put to flight by an angel (Dávila Padilla 1955, 615-16). One man from a town near Tlaxcala reported that he was brought to judgment, where he saw demons who wanted to take his soul, while angels defended it, until Saint James drove off the demons and the man regained consciousness (Mendieta 1980, 464). A woman of Culiacan, reviving as her body was about to be carried to church, told of appearing at judgment before an angry Christ, who sent her back to warn the people of her province to listen to the word of God and obey it (Mendieta 1980, 465).

In some cases the person's actual death was scheduled in the course of these visions. This is a European motif, seen for example in a Nahuatl narrative, based on a story recorded by Saint Gregory, of a garrulous young girl to whom the Virgin appears with a promise to take her to heaven in a month if she will stop talking so much (*Sermones y santoral en mexicano* n.d., 315r-v; Burkhart 2001). Other Nahuas also predicted their deaths, sometimes first preaching to relatives or neighbors to reform their sinful ways before it was too late for them (Mendieta 1980, 454-57). One young girl of Mexico City, apparently healthy, insisted on confessing to fray Alonso de Escalona, for her guardian angel had told her she would die that day, which she did, after foretelling, accurately, that her sister would die the next day (Mendieta 1980, 456). Such experiences, however much they resemble European models (and in the friars' retelling they may be molded further), suggest an attempt to exert control over the new, Christian representations of death and souls. At the same time, divine figures who tell a person when he or she will die also recall the traditional belief that deities such as the rain gods chose people to join them.

Death in Nahuatl Doctrinal Texts

Priests preaching in Nahuatl placed great emphasis on sin and its punishment, often presenting a simple dichotomy between heavenly reward and infernal torment. The seven mortal sins, the ten commandments of God, and the five commandments of the Church were to be memorized, and confession manuals organized their moral examinations around these lists. Hell is described sometimes in graphic detail, with its fires and its stenches, with its demons who, like Lucifer with his "metal warping frame" in "Final Judgment" and his sword in "The Life of Don Sebastián," torture the damned with assorted metal implements (Burkhart 1989, 54-56). On earth these demons are ever ready to tempt the unwary. The Augustinian fray Juan de la Anunciación warns of how they use food, pulque, women, and other temptations as bait, just like a fisherman uses a worm on a hook to deceive a fish (1577, 43v). When someone thinks about going to church, the demon comes to inspire bad thoughts, telling the person that going to church will serve no purpose and he or she will be hungry, thirsty, and cold (1577, 35v-36r). Demons beset women on their way to church in "The Life of Don Sebastián" and "Souls and Testamentary Executors."

As Lorenzo's wife in "How to Live on Earth" reminds her husband, Ash Wednesday was an occasion when priests encouraged people to contemplate their mortality. On this occasion, the Franciscan ethnographer fray Bernardino de Sahagún explains to his listeners that contemplation of death works like a medicine to keep them from sinning. He urges parents to admonish their children as follows:

> O my precious child, always remember that your life will come to an end, that you will die, and you do not know when, perhaps tomorrow, perhaps the day after. You will not remain here on earth for long. And when you die, if you lived well here on earth, and if you did penance on account of your sins, you will rest, you will rejoice in the home of God. But if you did not live well, if you die in your sins, when you die then your suffering will begin, so that you will suffer forever there in the place of the dead. (Sahagún 1563, 29r)[3]

He goes on to explain how death came to humanity as punishment for the sin of Adam and Eve. Later in the sermon, incorporating the day's biblical text from Genesis 3:19, Sahagún explains that the purpose of the ashes is "so that you will remember your being judged, your being sentenced, your death, for your mother Holy Church says to you, 'You person, you who are my child, may you remember that you are dust, and you will become dust again'" (29v). Everyone is made of earth, and all must humble themselves and do penance. The listeners are told that they should not love their bodies, for they are just earth, the food of worms; instead they should care for their souls (30r).

Fray Juan de la Anunciación, in his Ash Wednesday sermons, urges people to do penance during Lent; the ashes are to remind them that they themselves are earth and mud. Even one who is high-ranking and noble will become earth at death and should consign his or her body to the earth, for it will become the food of worms. The soul is what should be treasured, for it is not ash and earth but the image of God (1577, 39v). The Franciscan fray Alonso de Escalona, on the same occasion, tells sinners that God is angry at them because of their sins. They must turn toward God so that he will save their spirits (*-yolia*) from his judgment (*itetlatzontequililiz*) (n.d., 156v). As long as they are still alive, the demon cannot take them, and they still have a chance to turn their lives around and do penance for their sins. We should judge ourselves on earth so that we are not judged when we die, for sinners who do not save themselves from God's judgment while they still live on earth are sentenced to the fires of *mictlan* (Escalona n.d., 157v, 158v).

The souls of saints were sometimes observed to proceed directly to heaven, as do the souls of Saints Francis and Martin of Tours in Sahagún's *Psalmodia christiana* (1993b, 308–9, 334–35). But ordinary Nahuas virtuous enough to escape damnation could not expect so immediate a reward. A sojourn in purgatory was their more likely fate. To this place, as the mestizo priest don Bartolomé de Alva succinctly states:

> go the souls of those baptized Christians who did not provide satisfaction here on earth [with] their penance, for they are still to bring it to a conclusion. God gives them a penance of fire, there to quickly prepare and purify themselves during the time He has set down for them. (Sell and Schwaller 1999, 87)[4]

34—DEATH AND LIFE IN COLONIAL NAHUA MEXICO

Mural painting of purgatory from the open chapel of the Augustinian establishment at Actopan, Hidalgo. Souls languish in the flames, while a fortunate few depart with the assistance of angels. Photograph by Louise M. Burkhart.

Visual representations of purgatory seemingly were rare in colonial Mexico, but an example from the open chapel at Actopan, Hidalgo, shows the souls in flames. Ladders lead up from the flames, along which angels convey souls fortunate enough to have earned their release.

In his sermon on the Passion of Christ, Sahagún provides a more detailed exposition on the soul's fate after death. In Christ's case, the demon was waiting to carry off his soul, thinking that Christ was only a man, not a deity. But when Christ's soul emerged, his divine nature was visible, and the demon realized who he was and became frightened. Christ then seized him and chained him up in his home in the place of the dead (Sahagún 1563, 51r–v). This differs from an ordinary person's experience:

> All of us, when our soul emerges, the demon is waiting for it. And our soul, when it sees him, is very frightened, very scared, because the demon is very frightening, very scary. But our lord there comforts and strengthens his precious ones, his friends. And when our soul has emerged then it is taken before the Justice (*Justicia*) of God, in order to be accused, in order to be judged. And as for the Justice of God, it is very frightening. There is absolutely nothing like it. It overlooks absolutely nothing, even if it is just a little sin, called venial. It arranges the punishment of everything. Thus our soul is very frightened and scared when it is taken before the Justice of God. (51v)

A specific punishment is ordained for each particular sin, great or small. But then Jesus Christ speaks on behalf of his followers, saying: "'My suffering, which I endured, I assign to them, in order that they be rescued from the Justice of God. If it is necessary that they be flogged, that they be slapped in the face, on account of their sins, I myself was flogged, I was slapped in the face.' The suffering of our lord becomes the payment for his friends, his precious ones." (51v) When someone dies who has confessed a mortal sin but has not completed the assigned penances, he or she must go to purgatory:

> On account of each mortal sin he or she will do penance for seven years. Such is the command that the Justice of God established. On account of all of his or her sins, perhaps it will be 400[5] years. But to the Holy Church, by God's order, belongs Indulgence. Indulgence derives from the Passion, the suffering of our lord, which is the foundation stone of the Holy Church. Thus he or she will not go to purgatory. Thus it is evident how greatly he helps people, he consoles people with his Passion, with his death. So it is necessary that we be very grateful, and that we remember it every day. (52r)

This Passion-oriented account presents Christ as the principal intercessor on behalf of the dead, before an impersonalized "Justice." People are obliged to carry out penances in purgatory, but the text notes how indulgences can lessen one's term there.

However, it was Mary rather than Christ who was most often represented as the sinner's advocate, beseeching a judgmental Christ to have mercy on people's souls. The Tridentine reformed breviary of 1568 codified her role in the drama of death by standardizing the last line of the Hail Mary prayer as "pray for us sinners now and at the hour of our death" (Graef 1963–1965, 1:230–31). This was rendered into Nahuatl in different ways, including "may you speak for us sinners now and when our life on earth is about to end" (Anunciación 1575, 232–33) and "we sinners beseech you, may you speak for us before God now and when we are on the verge of death" (Sahagún 1993b, 24–25). She appears in this intercessory role on behalf of the dead in "How to Live on Earth," "The Life of Don Sebastián," and "Souls and Testamentary Executors." In "How to Live on Earth," it is to Mary that Lorenzo and his wife direct their prayers on behalf of the dead, prayers that may be understood to be rosaries, as later in the play Christ describes these good dead as people who pleased him by praying the rosary.

The anonymous Dominican *doctrina* of 1548, in a sermon on souls, describes the four sections of *mictlan* as being like huge houses (*yn iuhqui cenca ueuei calli*). These are the inferno of the damned (represented as a house in "The Life of Don Sebastián" and "Souls and Testamentary Executors"), the limbo of unbaptized children, purgatory, and the now-vacant limbo of the Holy Fathers (*Doctrina* 1944, 120r–22r). The third "house" is described as follows:

> There go those who sinned on earth, who did not keep the commands of God, but because of their sins they were very sad, they wept very much, and they confessed their sins before the heart-straightener.[6] Or perhaps they did not confess because it was not possible, but they wanted very much to straighten their hearts. Or they did not complete their penances here on earth. Therefore they go there to purgatory. Our great ruler, God, casts them there in order that there they complete what they did not do on earth on account of their sins. (121r)

In purgatory these souls must endure great suffering, but people on earth can help them by performing works of mercy, by fasting, and by praying for them.

> And the thing that is most helpful is the mass, when mass is said for them, perhaps one, or perhaps two, or perhaps many of the masses that are said for the souls in purgatory. The reason why it is a very great prayer, the mass is quite surpassing, is because our precious rescuer, Jesus Christ, who is truly God and truly man, is there when mass is said. And when we help the dead we will act prudently, for first we will help our fathers, or perhaps our mothers or perhaps our children, our wives, our grandfathers, or perhaps our relatives, our uncles, our aunts, or perhaps our friends and others who were baptized here on earth. (121v–122r)

However, one should not waste one's effort trying to help those who were never baptized, for they cannot be saved (122r).

This passage neatly summarizes the needs of the dead and the obligations of the living, an important theme in "How to Live on Earth" and "Souls and Testamentary Executors." The idea that it is useless to pray for the damned appears also in a miracle narrative in which an abbess who has been praying for the soul of her niece, a nun, is taken by Mary on a tour of hell. She sees her niece's soul being tortured in hell because of failure to confess a sexual sin; the aunt then prays for her no more (*Doctrina* n.d., 22v–24r; Burkhart 1999, 99–100).

Service to the dead was also taught through the fourteen works of mercy, comprising seven corporal and seven spiritual acts, which some Nahuatl catechisms list. The seventh corporal work of mercy is to bury the dead, an act the two good youths in "How to Live on Earth" perform for Lorenzo and his wife. Fray Juan de la Anunciación (1575, 204) describes this as an obligation not only to bury the dead but to join any funeral procession one sees and pray for the deceased's soul. One must not perform any old-time, non-Christian acts on the grave. The friar then declares that death is with everyone and draws one toward the tomb every day. Some live a long time and some do not, but everyone's life will end. Death "is not some omen, or something that is seen in a dream, nor is it something alive, nor is it like you see it painted, and it is not a cranium, a skull; death is with each person" (205). Friars considered the introduction of Christian burial rites a fundamental aspect of evangelization, as fray Diego Valadés suggested by placing a funeral procession in his idealized depiction of the Franciscan mission.

The seventh spiritual work of mercy, though it could be simply stated as an obligation to pray for everyone (*Códice franciscano* 1941, 45), more often was elaborated to encourage prayers for the dead (Anunciación 1565, 38v; Anunciación 1575, 207; and 1577, 263v). Fray Pedro de Gante's 1553 *doctrina* states that, even more than for the living, we should pray for the dead, whose souls God placed in purgatory, so that God will have mercy on them and take them up to heaven (Gante 1981, 63r). In the Dominican *doctrina*, Nahuas are told to help living people to know and serve God, but also to help the dead. Purgatory is here described as a prison and a place of suffering greater than that caused by syphilis, leprosy, or any other sickness on earth. Fires here on earth are like painted pictures compared to the fire of purgatory. The

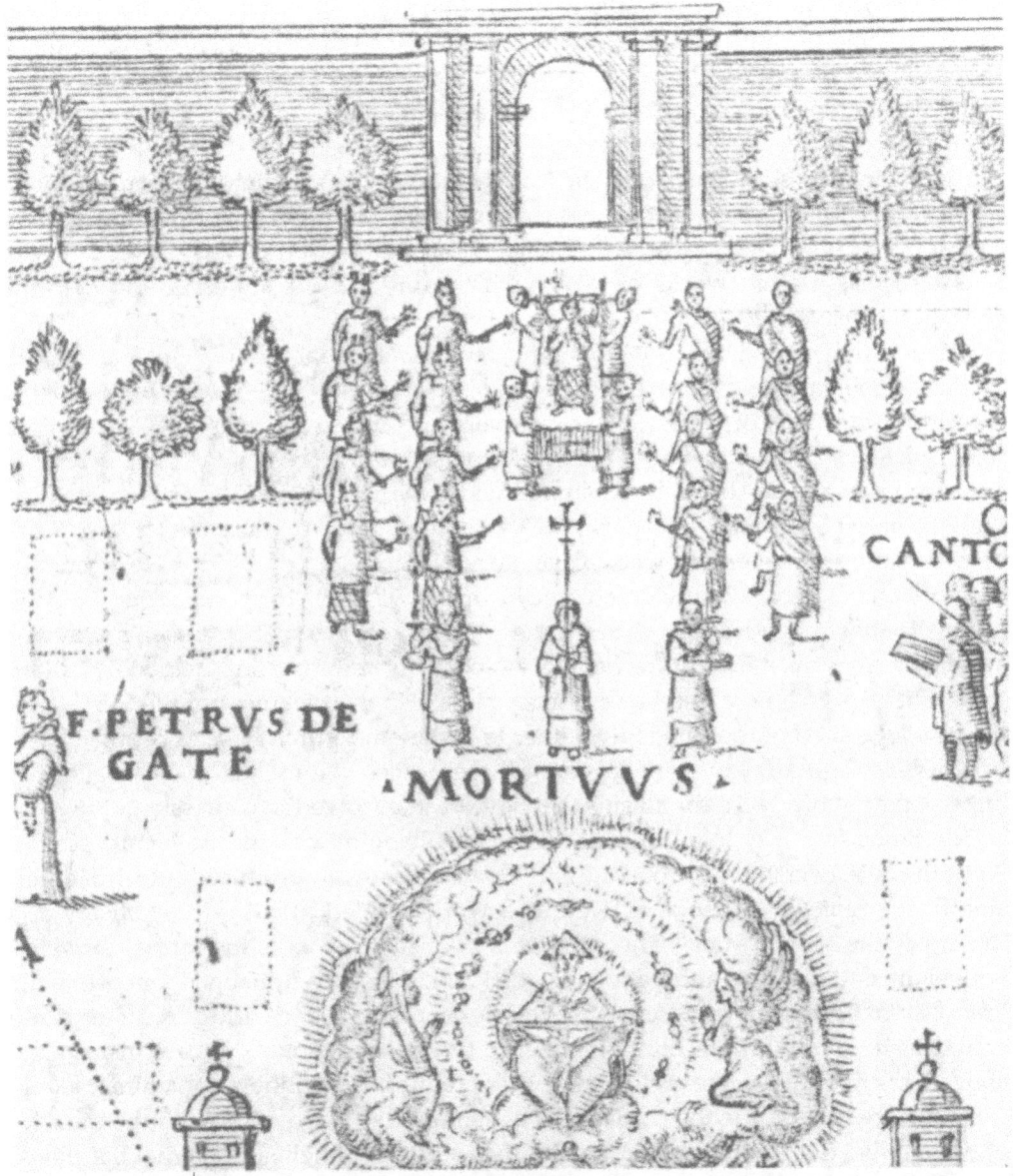

Detail from an engraving by fray Diego Valadés showing Franciscans and native Mexicans within an idealized church *atrio*. Here, a funeral procession enters the churchyard. Courtesy of the John Carter Brown Library at Brown University.

passage ends, "Therefore, oh my precious children, may you help the dead so that you may be helped" (*Doctrina* 1944, 118v–19v).

Fray Juan de la Anunciación (1575, 207–8) explains that, in regard to the dead, one should pray only for those who died in baptism and good deeds of the faith, whose souls may be doing penance in purgatory for their sins. One should not pray for innocent baptized children or for saints, for they are already in heaven. "Likewise," he adds, "one must not pray to our lord God for the people of long ago, the idolaters, who were your ancestors, who died in their blindness. They were not baptized, nor did they know the faith of our lord God. They went straight to the place of the dead, to make their homes there forever" (208–9). Unbaptized children cannot be released from the darkness of limbo (209). He then explains that purgatory is a place of torment where go the souls of believing Christians who did not do all the necessary penance for their sins. Purgatory means "the soul's place of complete purification" *(ycenquizcachipahualoyan yn anima)*, where souls are purified so they can go to heaven. The souls in that fiery place can be helped through various good deeds, prayers, offerings, masses, and works of mercy, which diminish the suffering and help the souls get to heaven (209–10).

Friars sought to extend to Nahuas the benefits of papal jubilees—plenary indulgences occasionally granted to anyone who performed a specified series of devotional acts, including fasts, prayers, alms, confession, and taking communion. These eliminated whatever debt of time in purgatory the person had accrued up to then. In his *confessionario mayor*, fray Alonso de Molina provides two sets of instructions for attaining these plenary indulgences (1984, 95v–98r). Fray Juan de la Anunciación (1575, 148–52) provides one set, preceded by an explanatory discourse on purgatory. Here the friar notes that no one knows how much time he or she will have to spend in purgatory. In order that one may escape it entirely, the Church keeps "what in a sacred way is a very great treasure, a benefit for people, which is the suffering and merits of our lord Jesus Christ, which he earned as a human man, also the penances of the Saints. It is the privilege and boon of the Holy Father to assign and grant these to people" (150). Whenever he does so, by carrying out all the pope's commands one can gain full remission of punishment for all sins that have been absolved in confession.

The Franciscan fray Juan Bautista Viseo, in collaboration with the Nahua scholar Agustín de la Fuente and probably other Nahuas as well, produced a Nahuatl version of the *contemptus mundi* as well as a work entitled "Book of the Misery and Brevity of the Life of Man." The latter was published in 1604; the former survives, with eighteenth-century annotations by the Franciscan fray Agustín Vetancurt, in the John Carter Brown Library. As such esoteric works of otherworldly contemplation would have found a more limited audience than the sermons and catechisms cited above, I restrict my comments to a few observations on the published volume.

Its five treatises guide the reader on a contemplative journey through the miseries of human life, death, the final judgment, the torments of hell, and eternal happiness in paradise. The treatise on death emphasizes the frightening nature of death, the tomb, the dead body, and all that happens to the dying and dead person. By contemplating death one may gain the wisdom to govern one's life, the resolve to abandon sin, and the foresight to prepare for a good death *(inic qualli yectli ipan micohuaz*, "so that one will die in the good, the proper" [Bautista 1604, 38v–45r]). Just as soldiers drill for battle, so should we examine the pathways we will follow in death, "for no one can see death, and the road that is followed is very dark, quite dangerous, quite rocky, as we all know, and full of destruction and danger. One who falls will not be able to rise again, but will go falling into the abyss, the place of the dead, Hell" (44v). When the soul comes out from the body, it follows an unknown road to a new land, beset by frightening things and the shadow of death, dependent for help on its guardian angel, threatened by wild beasts (70r–v). Even more frightening is the judgment it will undergo, in the presence of judge, accusers, and defenders, as each deed is recounted and the sentence is pronounced (70v–72r). How will it be, the text asks, if you are condemned forever? You will know great pain and suffering. "But how your enemies will rejoice, will delight, will consider it a festival, will celebrate a festival. They will really gloat over you, they will laugh at you" (72r).

Texts on the Final Judgment

The Final Judgment drama presents another afterlife scenario, enacting what happens when Christ returns, the dead come back to life, and people are consigned to their permanent destinations. Christ's return as judge was proclaimed in the seventh Article of Faith pertaining to Christ's humanity, *Inde venturus est judicare vivos et mortuos* (whence [from heaven] he will come to judge the living and the dead). Nahuas would have learned of the final judgment principally from explanations of this article, which was part of the basic catechism. It was also the subject of a number of Indo-Christian artistic works—in both relief sculpture, as on a *posa* chapel at San Andrés Calpan, Puebla, and mural painting, as in the large open chapel at Actopan, Hidalgo.

The 1548 Dominican *doctrina* (*Doctrina* 1944, 126v–28r), explaining the seventh article of faith, describes how at the end of the world everyone will die but will then come back to life in the bodies that they have now. Everyone will gather in the Valley of Jehosaphat, near Jerusalem, to be judged.[7] Jesus Christ will come down in his human form to judge the good and the bad. "And he will interrogate each one, and he will inquire as to what they did, and what they said, and what they thought, what they coveted, and what they neglected through laziness while they still lived here on earth" (127r). He will start with the popes and work his way down through the ecclesiastical hierarchy, then the rulers and lords and their wives, those who are indigenous people (*nican tlaca*, "people here") and Spaniards and people from everywhere in the world, and then the common people from all over the world. All the sins everyone did—and all the good things everyone did—will be revealed. He will take the good people to his royal home in heaven, body and soul, and the bad ones he will cast into the place of the dead, or hell, body and soul.

Gante's 1553 *doctrina* (1981, 30r–32v) tells how Christ will give all people what they deserve, in accordance with their deeds, although here he does not interrogate them. The people will be divided into four groups, two to be damned and two to be saved:

> The first ones to be judged are those who just took the faith in vain, who just believed in our lord God in vain, who did not carry out with their lives what they said, "I believe in our lord Jesus Christ, who is our precious rescuer, our deity, our ruler." And even though they said this with their mouths they did not live according to his sacred commands, they were like bad Christians. Even though sometimes they did good things, they died in mortal sin. The way they will be judged is that they will be scorned, they will be cast into the place of the dead. The second ones who will be judged are the true Christians, who lived according to what is good and proper, who worried about their sins, who died in penance and penitence. They will be judged with compassion, they will be rescued, they will be given eternal happiness in heaven.

Native artist's relief sculpture on one of the *posa* chapels at the Franciscan establishment of San Andrés Calpan, Puebla. Christ sits in judgment, flowers to his right and sword to his left, flanked by angels and attended by Mary and John the Baptist. The dead rise from their graves. Photograph by Louise M. Burkhart.

The third group contains those hopeless cases who never even believed in Christ, while those in the fourth group are so good that they will judge others rather than being judged themselves. To these privileged souls Jesus Christ said, "You will place yourselves with me on twelve golden thrones so that you also will judge the people of Israel."[8] Christ will invite the two good groups to take the eternal happiness that has been waiting for them since the world began. But to the accursed he will say:

> "You accursed ones, you never believed in me, and you did not serve me. And you died in your sins, your wickedness. Go, so that you will never see me. Get away from me, you accursed ones. You will be tied up forever there in the fiery oven, in the middle of the fire. You will never rest. May you fully take your utter suffering, your burning, which will never ever come to an end. You will never be able to escape. You will always remain shut up there with the demons whom you served, whom you obeyed. May you suffer with them. Suffering is waiting for you there."

Detail from a mural painting of the Final Judgment in the open chapel at Actopan, Hidalgo. While an angel blows a trumpet, dead people rise from their graves. In the foreground, one is accosted by a demon while an angel attends another. Photograph by Louise M. Burkhart.

Then the earth will stretch open its mouth and swallow up the damned with the demons.[9] Christ will lead the saved ones to heaven, accompanied by music and song.

In his 1575 *doctrina* (54–66), fray Juan de la Anunciación describes how God will come to examine *(quimmotlatemoliliquiuh)* all people about what they said, did, thought, and desired in regard to the sacred commands, rewarding those who kept his commands and punishing those who did not. He distinguishes between the individual judgment *(tetlatzōtequililiztli yn tetech pouhtica)* that everyone undergoes when his or her soul has departed and the final, universal judgment *(tecentzonquizcatlatzontequililiztli)*, when all people will die and be judged in front of one another. All will be assembled and Christ will descend from heaven to the place of judgment, up in the air. He will have the angels place the good on his right hand and the bad on his left.[10] To the good he will explain how all the kind acts they performed for the poor, sick, or hungry were also done for him. He will escort them to heaven; a description of its delights follows. Then he will return to harangue the bad, with specific reference to works of mercy that they failed to perform:

> How wretched you are! You have failed, you have cursed yourselves, you have destroyed yourselves with sin. Listen to your blind deeds. Truly you joyfully

pursued earthliness, and you obeyed your bodies, you did anything that demanded you to sin, you served the worthless demons. And you did not keep my commands for me, nor did you obey my admonitions. I went about among you naked, but you did not clothe me with pity, and I went about starving, but you did not feed[11] me with pity, you did not give me water with pity, and I was sick, I was imprisoned, but you did not visit me with pity, so my heart did not rest through your consolation, and when I was a vagabond you did not house me with pity. (60–61)

A similar reproach appears in "The Life of Don Sebastián." Then Christ will consign them to hell. The earth will break open in their midst and they will roll down, bumping from crag to crag, until they reach their fiery home in the place of the dead. A description of hell completes the exposition of the article.

The same fray Juan de la Anunciación presents a slightly different account in the catechism appended to his 1577 *Sermonario* (238v–39v). He tells how a great fire will purify the earth. Then (as in Luke 21:25–26) the sun will go dark, the moon will cease to shine, the stars will fall from the sky, and the people will fall into great dismay. By the power of God all will revive to be judged. Those who had good lives will be pure and will outshine the sun; the bad will be frightful and blacker than the night. Even though each of us is judged individually when we die, unwitnessed by other people, this judgment will be done publicly. But rather than describing an interrogation, this friar says "our lord God will create, will make, a light, which very quickly will reveal everything that each person thought, everything he or she said, everything he or she did, all the time that he or she lived." Then Christ will judge everyone, giving rulership in heaven to the good people who had pity on the poor and kept his commands. The bad will be cast into the place of the dead to burn forever in the fires.

Churchgoers also heard priests sermonizing about the end of the world on the first Sunday in Advent, for which the Gospel text was a passage in Luke (21:25) where Jesus speaks of the signs in the heavens and turbulence on earth that will precede the coming of the Son of Man in glory and the redemption. Sahagún, in his sermon for this week, tells how the people will revive and be divided, the good at Christ's right hand and the bad at his left. He will invite the good ones to take their kingdom and they will enter heaven. The bad ones he will consign to the flames of the place of the dead (Sahagún 1563, 1v). Fray Juan de la Anunciación describes the destruction of the world in considerable detail, then the individual sinner's frightening experiences: the gaping mouth of hell will be trying to suck you in, demons will prepare to throw you down into the fire, you will see all your sins and bad deeds threatening you and accusing you before God. No one will be able to help you, nor will you be able to hide: you will have to stand by yourself before God. Anunciación then urges his listeners to look ahead and prepare themselves for judgment (1577, 3v–4r).

Fray Juan Bautista and his Nahua collaborators wrote three sermons on this gospel text (Bautista 1606, 121–248). The first two deal with the signs of the end of the world, while the third recounts in detail, with many parables and biblical references, the coming of Christ as judge and the final judgment. The sermon compares the last judgment to a court trial on earth, with judge, accused, accusers, witnesses, and a place for the trial to occur. Fortunately for humanity, the judge will be Christ, who will be merciful. All people will come back to life, even if they died very long ago, and all their good and bad deeds will be manifested. No one will be able to hide from the judge. Accusers and witnesses will include each person's own conscience (*ineyoliximachiliz*, "knowledge of one's heart"), all of God's creations, everyone's own sins, and Lucifer and the other demons. The good will be placed at Christ's right hand and he will call them to take possession of the kingdom of heaven. The bad will go to his left, and in anger he will consign them to the fires of *mictlan*. The torments of hell are detailed, including the demons' delight in causing their prisoners to suffer in the stinking, black, and dirty fires. It will be the angels who carry out Christ's judgment, and even the Virgin Mary will be unable to intercede on behalf of the condemned. The end of the sermon stresses that knowledge of this final reckoning leads prudent people to avoid sin.

Bautista also devoted the third treatise of his contemplative work "Book of the Misery and Brevity of the Life of Man" to the final judgment (1604, 72v–102v). The treatise has four chapters. The first focuses on the frightful nature of the judgment, the second (like the first two sermons in his 1606 book) on the signs that the day is coming, the third on the destruction of the world and the resurrection of the dead, and the fourth on the coming of the judge and the judgment itself, with its accusers and witnesses.

Nahuatl Wills

Separation of the self into spirit and flesh was emphasized when people dictated their last will and testament. This activity, highlighted in "Souls and Testamentary Executors" and "The Merchant," was considered an essential component of a good death. Colonial Nahuas' participation in this custom resulted in a large corpus of documents, which is enormously important for reconstructing many facets of colonial Nahua social and economic life (Cline 1986; Cline and León-Portilla 1984; Horn 1998; Kellogg 1998; Lockhart 1992; Wood 1991, 1998). Perhaps as much as or even more than formal preaching, will-making familiarized Nahuas with Catholic practices and discourse related to death. Friars provided model wills in Nahuatl, such as the published examples offered by the Franciscan fray Alonso de Molina in his *confessionario mayor*, first published in 1565 (Molina 1984; see Cline 1998) and the Dominican fray Martín de León in his 1611 *Camino del cielo* (1611); native notaries mastered the proper formulas for recording them. As statements of faith, wills are somewhat problematic: notaries tended to write down similar standardized pious formulas that may not correspond to actual declarations by the dying person, and elaborate invocations may index elite display rather than intense indoctrination (Cline 1998, 24–25; Lockhart 1992, 251–54). However, more personal statements do appear, and even the most formulaic wills indicate that people were conversant with the concepts and considered their inscription appropriate and necessary.

Testamentary statements related to beliefs about death fall mainly into two categories: the encommendation (Eire 1995, 36), in which testators' consign their souls to God and their bodies to burial; and a subsequent statement, in which they bequeath money or goods to pay for masses for their souls in purgatory. Some also make arrangements for their funerals. The basic formula for the encommendation imposes a dualist division between soul (called *-yolia, ánima,* or frequently both) and body (*-nacayo,* "flesh," or the "earth, mud" diphrase) as the components of the human self relevant in the context of death. Fray Alonso de Molina's model testament suggests the following wording for this part:

> First of all, I place my soul in the hands of our lord God, for he made it, and I beseech him to have compassion for me, to pardon my sins for me, to take me to his home in heaven (when my soul has left my body). And my body I consign to the earth for thence it came. It is earth, it is mud. And I want only a mantle with which it will be wrapped in order to be buried. And I want it to be buried there in our church of Saint Anthony of Padua, where the priest will indicate for me my sepulcher, my tomb, my burial place (Molina 1984, 61v; Cline 1998, 28).

Fray Martín de León's model proposes the following:

> Now first of all I leave my soul in the hands of our lord Jesus Christ, because he made it, he rescued it with his precious blood, with his death on the holy cross. And my trunk,[12] my body, I consign to the earth, because thence it came, of it it was made. I also command that when God wants me to die, my earthly body will be buried there in the church-home of God, in the home of Saint N. here in the altepetl N. wherever my priest will bury me, in my burial place. And so that I will be buried there I make an offering of N. peso(s). (1611, 139v)

Most Nahuatl wills have some statement analogous to these. Some samples will indicate the range of variation.[13] One of the earliest Nahuatl wills yet published is that of Mexico City's María Tiacapan, from 1561, who stated, "And I say that my deity, my ruler made my soul and I go place it in his hands and I say that all my children, you who are here beside me, I order you not to forget me. May you always pray to our lord on behalf of my soul" (Reyes García et al. 1996, 282). The 1566 will of don Julián de la Rosa, a Tlaxcalan nobleman, gives a more formulaic statement:

> First I entrust my soul to God, the all-powerful, who created it, who rescued it with his precious blood. And my body I give to the earth because thence it came. If this is a sickness from which my body will die, I want to be buried there in the church of Saint Mary in Tlaxcala, in front of the crucifix. (Anderson et al. 1976, 44–45)

Martín Jacobo's 1577 will from Mexico City states, after the customary invocation of the Trinity:

> The first of my words that I say is that if I die I place my spirit, my soul, entirely in his hands. May he take it for it is his creation, it is his rescued thing. May he carry it to his home in heaven. And my body is earth, is the food of worms. And when I have died I will be buried here in [the church of] Saint Mary in the barrio of Quauhtepec. (Reyes García et al. 1996, 170)

This statement by Miguel Chimaltecuhtli, from 1580, is typical of the corpus of sixty-five wills from Culhuacan:

> First I say that I give my spirit, my soul, to our lord God because he made it and he came to rescue it with his blood here on earth. And my body I give to the earth because thence it came. And when my soul has come out my body will go to be buried at our church of Saint John the Evangelist. (Cline and León-Portilla 1984, 46–47)

However, fellow Culhuacan resident Juana Tiacapan, also dying in 1580, did not distinguish her spiritual from her physical fate: "When I die, may our lord God carry me to himself, because he is the rescue of my soul, it is his image. And may my angel, my guardian, carry me before God" (Cline and León-Portilla 1984, 66–67).

In 1596 Juana Mocel of Mexico City dictated:

> First of all I go place my soul in the hands of our lord God for he made it. And I beseech him to pardon me my sins with which I offended him all the time that I lived here on earth, so that he will come to carry me to his home in heaven when my soul has abandoned my body. (Reyes García et al. 1996, 274)

A will from 1617 gives this statement:

> And now our lord God has placed his justice (*justicia*) upon me. My name is Juan Fabián, my home is here in San Bartolomé Atenco, still of my own will I establish my testament, since my earth, my mud has grown old. I am just waiting for the word of my precious father, God, when he will pass judgment on me, so that I will leave the earth. If our lord God destroys me I place my spirit, my soul, in his hands because it is his rescued thing, he rescued it. And my earth, my mud belongs to the earth because thence it came, for I will become earth and mud. May our lord God just take my spirit, my soul, for I give it entirely to him. (Anderson et al. 1976, 58–59)

Justina Xochicuetzin, a Tlaxcalan colonist in San Esteban de la Nueva Tlaxcala (now in Coahuila), planned this death in 1627:

> First of all I place my soul in the hands of our lord God and I beseech him to have compassion for me, to pardon me for my sins. May he take me before him in heaven when my soul has abandoned my body and I beseech the eternally maiden Saint Mary to speak for me before her precious child when I am on the verge of death, also Saint Peter, Saint Paul, and Saint Francis, so that they will speak for me before God. And my body I consign to the earth for thence it came, it is earth, it is mud, and I want just a mantle with which it will be wrapped in order to be buried. Where I used to sit [in church?], there my body will be buried. (Offutt 1992, 426–27)

Don Agustín Miguel, from San Bartolomé Capuluac in the Toluca Valley, shows even more concern for his soul in his will, dictated sometime after 1634. He prays that he may happily receive what God has sent him, "your scorpion, your nettle," that is, his illness. He continues:

> I place my spirit, my soul, entirely in his hands. May he receive it happily, for I am a sinner, I have offended him with many things, I am a great, 400-times sinner, which they (devils? angels?) will remember about me. So that he will love me, truly I will repay God's death. Now it is time, now it is the moment that my accounting *(notlapoal)* arrives, by which I will go to give an account *(cuetan)* to God. As for my earthly body, at the feet of my precious father Holy Saint Bartholomew I will be buried. (Wood 1998, 104–5)

In 1661 Agustina Juana of Coyoacan declared:

> God has placed his justice *(justicia)* upon me, a sickness. My earth, my mud is quite heavy, but there is nothing wrong with my soul. If my ruler, God, wants me, I place entirely in his hands my spirit, my soul, since it is his creation, his rescued thing. . . . When I have died I will be buried at the foot of my precious father Saint John the Baptist [the main Coyoacan church]. I will be buried there in front of Our Lady of the Transit. (Horn 1998, 78)

As late as 1776, Nahuas such as don Felix Martín Ramos of San Esteban produced wills with similar formulas:

> This is first of all, that I leave my soul in the hands of our lord God, since it is his creation and through [his] death he rescued it on the holy cross. And my earthly body I consign to the earth for from it it was made. I also declare that when God wants me to die I request that my earthly body be buried in the church-home of our lord God Saint San Francisco, in front of the altar of our precious and honored mother of the Conception, wherever there will be a place. (Offutt 1992, 438–39)

Many Nahua testators refer to their soul by the Nahuatl as well as the Spanish term. Death is attributed to God. Some see their sickness or death as God's "justice" or judgment upon them; some express concern over sin. Being carried before God, even being judged and having to provide an "accounting" of oneself, are motifs in the morality plays that have also found their way into wills.

In the model wills, the above statements are followed immediately by bequests to help the deceased's soul shorten its stay in purgatory. Molina's model provides for a vigil and one or more masses "for the sake of the helping of my soul," to be said when the body is buried or, if not possible then, the following day (1984, 61v). León's testator, "in regard to the helping of my soul," leaves money for masses, the number to be specified in each case, and for the *teopan tlaca*, or native church attendants. These are to pray three *responsos*, or responses for the dead (chanted during "Souls and Testamentary Executors"), as they take the body to church and also "they will say vigil *(Vigilia)* over me" (1611, 139v). These requests follow Spanish custom under which testators often specified a certain number of pauses or *posas* on the way to church, when the pallbearers could rest and the clergy would intone a response (Eire 1995, 124–25). For the vigil, people gathered around the dead body to pray for a period before burial (Eire 1995, 121).

Nahua testators typically provide for their burial and masses through cash bequests or, more frequently, by ordering that certain property be sold to raise the needed funds. Juana Mocel ordered a house sold and a debt collected, assigning a total of ninety-five pesos to her burial and masses (Reyes García et al. 1996, 275). Other individuals whose wills are quoted above sought to help their souls with cash and the sale of fine clothing, a horse, a donkey, building stone, and crops in the field. María Tiacapan financed no masses but left money for three responses to be said for her in the main Tlatelolco church, encharging district officials present at her deathbed with seeing that this was done; annotations on her will indicate that it was. She also provided candles for all of her grandchildren to carry at her funeral, a shirt and a maguey-fiber shroud for her body, and money for the church singers and other funeral expenses (Reyes García et al. 1996, 282–83). Some testators left money to pay for the tolling of bells; for example, both Juan Fabián and Agustina Juana left money for the bells to be rung at four different churches (Anderson et al. 1976, 58–59; Horn 1998, 78–79). This tolling of bells for the dead appears in "Souls and Testamentary Executors." Martín Jacobo left fifteen pesos to buy masses for his parents and twenty pesos in alms for local churches, but he must have depended on his heirs to finance masses for his own soul (Reyes García et al. 1996, 171).

Such death-related bequests represented a significant transfer of property from indigenous families to the Church. People must have considered the financing of masses for their souls a serious obligation. Although requiem masses might also serve as commemorative rites and a source of prestige, people presumably understood that the masses' principal purpose was to benefit the soul in purgatory, and thus in dictating their wills people assumed that their souls would pass through this place rather than proceeding directly to heaven or undergoing damnation. Otherwise, there was little point in imposing this financial burden on their heirs. These requested masses were, indeed, not always performed, whether as a result of greed, indifference, poverty, or a feeling that "the dying man or woman had overdone it in the moment of extremity" (Lockhart 1992, 214). Still, to have at least one mass said was seen as a serious obligation, although sometimes even this was not carried out as quickly as the deceased might have wished, the executor sometimes dying beforehand and financing the neglected masses through his or her own will (Lockhart 1992, 214; also León-Portilla and Cline 1984, and Anderson et al. 1976, 64–65). *Fiscales*, the highest-ranking indigenous religious officials, often served as executors and were also responsible for receiving the payments for the masses; overzealous execution of this office could lead to conflicts over the handling of estates (Lockhart 1992, 213–15).

Care of the Dying and the Dead

A proper Spanish death was attended by a priest, who would administer the sacrament of extreme unction, exhort and pray for the dying person, and help to keep at bay the demons who were thought to lurk about the deathbed (Eire 1995, 29–32). Most Nahuas, however, probably died without a priest at their bedside. Cline observes that none of the Culhuacan wills were witnessed by any of the local Augustinians (1986, 21). During the early years, the friars were too busy ensuring that the most vital sacraments were delivered, but eventually the sacrament of extreme unction (or the last rites) did become available to Nahuas who requested it—and who lived close enough to a priest to be able to call one to a loved one's deathbed or carry the sick person to the church (Mendieta 1980, 307).

Some Nahuatl catechisms mention this sacrament only briefly (*Códice franciscano* 1941, 39; Anunciación 1565, 28v; Gante 1981, 58v; Sahagún 1993b, 30–31). Fray Juan de la Anunciación's 1577 catechism explains that it is to be administered to adults who are in danger of dying (260v–61r). His 1575 version (162–65) explains that God places goodness *(qualtiliztli)* in the sacrament, with which peoples' souls are helped. The priest anoints with holy oil each of the sick person's five senses. The sick person, after confessing, must ask the priest for the sacrament humbly, saying, "O my precious father, if my sickness increases, if I become very ill, may your heart grant that you will give me as my gift the sacrament, the sacred anointing and marking *(teoyotica teoçaliztli temachiotiliztli)*." It is the responsibility of people in the sick person's household to bring him or her to the church; this implies that the Augustinians did not make house calls.[14] An admonition to console the sick person encourages him or her to trust in God, who does not want his or her soul to be lost but to take it to heaven, even if it is not deserving, and to receive his or her approaching death gladly. Don Bartolomé de Alva's 1634 confession manual presents a similar admonition, in which the dying person is encouraged to be brave and to be sure to confess anything that is troubling him or her so as not to present God with a dirty soul (Sell and Schwaller 1999, 153).

But even Nahuas who faced this crucial moment without priestly attention were given some resources to assist them in their passage. The Franciscan fray Pedro de Gante (1981, 151r–58v) and the Dominican fray Martín de León (1611, 141r–54v) adapted the *Ars moriendi,* or guidebook for dying well, into Nahuatl, with admonitions, questions, and prayers for the dying and instructions on the treatment of the dying person and the corpse.[15] Such guidebooks supplement will-making by introducing additional European death customs into Nahua homes.

Gante's guide, a section of his widely used *doctrina* of 1553, is titled, "Here is how each person who is a true Christian will prepare, when he or she is sick, so that he or she will die in the service of our lord Jesus Christ" (151r). Gante begins by recommending that whoever is caring for the person ascertain whether he or she has been baptized, and instructions on how to carry out this rite, which a lay person could perform in time of extremity, follow. Then additional questions verify the person's Christian beliefs, contrition for sin, desire for pardon, and so forth; the proper answer, "yes," is printed after each question. The final questions ask if the dying person prays to Mary and all the saints to speak for him or her before God, whether he or she asks that the Holy Church and all true Christians pray for him or her and help him or her before God, and whether he or she lays his or her death and suffering in the illness as an offering before God. There follows a series of prayers for the dying person to make to Christ, then a prayer to Mary, who is asked to ensure that the dying person will see Christ and will hear the angels calling to his[16] soul to come out and rejoice with them, and to help him so that his enemies—that is, the demons—will not afflict him.

Gante urges repetition of these prayers, the catechism, and the Passion of Christ. The latter could be done using the texts for the canonical hours printed elsewhere in Gante's book (132r–44r). An image of Christ should be placed before the dying person, holy water should be sprinkled about, and a candle that has been blessed should be placed in the person's hands when death is near. Those present should kneel and recite a long litany beseeching God to save the person and requesting the intercession of Mary and a list of other saints. Referencing non-Christian native practice, Gante cautions them not to kneel before or call to the dead "as is done in confusion" (that is, idolatry or heresy), or to make offerings to them "as it used to be done long ago." Anyone who does this will fall into serious sin (158r–v). The body will be wrapped in a white mantle. When they are about to bury it, a cross will go in front, before which they will kneel and pray the prayers Our Father and Hail Mary as offerings to God on behalf of the deceased's soul.

Fray Martín de León's bilingual *Arte de bien morir*, which follows his will-making instructions in the 1611 *Camino del cielo*, was intended for use by Nahuatl or Spanish speakers. It begins with four admonitions to the dying, urging acceptance of mortality, gratitude for the opportunity to prepare for death, acceptance of the attendant suffering as penance for sin, and the renunciation of earthly cares in order to focus on the divine. He or she should ask all those present to pray to God to have mercy on his or her soul, and should pray to Mary and to all the angels and saints, especially his or her own guardian angel and Saint Mary Magdalene, that they pray to God on his or her behalf. A series of questions follows. A priest is to be called if the person has any unconfessed sins. One question concerns the disposal of the person's goods and payment of debts and is to be followed by the making of the will. Then there is a series of prayers, to Christ, Mary, the angels, and any saint to whom the person was particularly devoted. Other instructions include the bringing of a crucifix, which the dying person is to kiss; signs of the cross made over the eyes, mouth, ears, nose, and heart to guard against demonic deceptions; the provision of a blessed candle with the seal of Our Lady; and other procedures required for certain indulgences (such as the Santa Cruzada). León also provides instructions for the proper arrangement and disposal of the body, emphasizing that whatever masses and alms the dead person provided for in the will should be carried out quickly so that he or she will not remain long in purgatory. God will punish negligent relatives and executors with suffering in hell—a threat that gets carried out in "Souls and Testamentary Executors."

Colonial Nahuas participated avidly in religious confraternities—voluntary sodalities that carried out devotional and charitable activities and provided leadership opportunities for indigenous men and women (Lockhart 1992, 218–29). Confraternities offered indulgences to their members in exchange for the execution of specific devotions. To Nahuas, gaining these indulgences may not have been a major motivation for joining a confraternity, but once they had done so they were drawn further into the Catholic system of toting up release time from purgatory. For example, members of the confraternity of the Most Holy Sacrament in Tula gained papal indulgences by attending, candles in hand, a special mass on the first Sunday of each month and on five Marian feast days and the feasts of Saints Joseph and Francis (Schwaller 1989, 241).

The copious papal indulgences enjoyed by members of the popular confraternity of the rosary were publicized in Spanish through local editions of such works as the

Dominican Hierónimo Taix's *Institución, modo de rezar, y milagros e indulgencias del Rosario de la virgen Maria* of 1576,[17] but also in Nahuatl. A 1572 translation of rosary indulgences into Nahuatl, by fray Alonso de Molina, was about to be published by the printer Pedro Ocharte when he was arrested (for other reasons) by the Inquisition; the work survives in a handwritten copy (*Doctrina* n.d., 108v–15v; Fernández del Castillo 1982, 85–141; Schwaller 1991, 313–15). Compilations of miracles associated with the rosary promised other death-related rewards. In one Nahuatl series (*Sermones y santoral en mexicano* n.d., 322v–28v), a young woman who belongs to the confraternity, after being attacked by a wolf, survives long enough to confess and receive the last rites, thus accomplishing a good death. Another young female confraternity member returns to life after drowning, once her mother reminds the Virgin that the girl was a rosary devotee and vows to join the confraternity herself. And another young woman devoted to the rosary, a poor shepherdess, enjoys a splendid death attended by the Virgin and other heavenly maidens. One local legend held that the Dominican fray Domingo de la Anunciación, by praying the rosary, was able to call back from death a man from Tepetlaoztoc who had died before the friar could come to confess him; after confessing, he died again (Dávila Padilla 1955, 615–16).

Confraternities assisted the dead and dying in more immediate ways as well. The Nahuatl statutes from Tula (Schwaller 1989, 241–43) call for a draped litter and two processional crosses to be used for any member's funeral. All members of the sodality, summoned by fifteen chimes of the church bell, are to march in the funeral procession. Spanish members (who did pay higher fees) are to receive vigils, masses, and responses at confraternity expense. Nahuas who wanted these things had, presumably, to pay for them themselves. For twice the normal membership fee, a dying person could join the confraternity and receive the death benefits and indulgences. But the confraternity also buried destitute residents of the community, whether or not they were members. Confraternity officers were to ensure that any sick member confessed and received communion, so that he or she would be prepared for a good death.

The 1619 statutes of San Miguel Coyotlan's confraternity of Our Lady of Solitude (Sell 2000, 354) call for similar attention to the dead and dying. When a member is ill, confraternity deputies must fetch a priest to hear his or her confession. Members must provide candles for the funerals of poor members and finance two low masses for them. The latter obligation extends even to poor people who do not belong to the sodality: members must pay for a mass if the person would otherwise receive none. That Nahua confraternities typically took seriously the obligation to provide masses for dead members is also indicated by the well-preserved colonial confraternity records from colonial Tecamachalco, which contain careful annotations regarding the masses performed for deceased members and the money spent on these (Annette McLeod, personal communication, 2000).

Some confraternities were explicitly dedicated to death and the dead. The Augustinians founded confraternities for the souls in purgatory at all of their establishments in Mexico; these sponsored weekly masses on Mondays for the souls of all the dead (Grijalva 1624, 72v). By the late seventeenth century, confraternities of the souls were common at Franciscan establishments as well, in some cases separate ones for Spaniards and natives (Vetancurt 1982). In 1710 the Jesuits founded a branch of their Good Death Society, dedicated to preparing its members for death through a well-regulated life, among the Nahuas of Mexico City; membership in this sodality also brought indulgences (Schroeder 2000).

Good Deaths and Bad

Most of the deaths that occur in the five plays, on or off stage, are disastrously bad deaths. The disrespectful youth in "How to Live on Earth," the greedy and lecherous protagonist of "The Merchant," and the widow and executors in "Souls and Testamentary Executors" are actually killed by demons, having sunk so low as to be beyond redemption. Doña Juana is murdered by her husband who, unshriven of this mortal sin, is then stoned to death. Lucía in "Final Judgment" does not die but receives eternal punishment at judgment time for failing to confess her sins before it was too late. All of these characters go to hell. Thus, on the whole the plays emphasize negative examples, modeling frightful fates that the prudent observer will strive to avoid. The torments enacted by demons visually reinforce teachings about hell delivered in sermons and catechism lessons.

The behaviors for which these characters earn such dire punishment were acts that most Nahuas already disapproved of. Even if some Nahuas in the audience did not consider the merchant's usury inherently sinful, they would have objected to his theft of a widow's property. Murder, adultery, promiscuity, drunkenness, and disrespect for parents were, like theft, sanctioned under preconquest as well as colonial moral codes. To colonial Nahuas familiar with wills, failure to arrange the masses funded by a dead person's will was also a serious breach. So, the moral lessons were not in themselves particularly rigid or alarming, even if the punishments were severe. To feel morally superior to the bad characters in the plays, and thus expect to avoid their fate and end up, at the worst, in purgatory, might not have seemed all that difficult, despite the bleak tone struck by many of the heavenly and allegorical characters.

Lorenzo and his wife of "How to Live on Earth" and don Pedro of "Souls and Testamentary Executors" die good deaths and proceed to purgatory. Don Pedro dies offstage, apparently just after he goes to church and makes his last confession, but the deaths of Lorenzo and his wife are staged. They die with no one to attend them, but even so their deaths have features of the good deaths prescribed by Gante and León. They have just confessed and they are at peace with one another and accepting of their fate. An angel calls to them and other souls come to help, bringing the candles that the dying person is supposed to hold and ushering the emerging souls to purgatory.

Aside from their participation in the sacrament of confession, the principal pious behavior attributed to these three characters is their own renunciation of earthly wealth in favor of service to the dead in purgatory. Lorenzo and his wife forego seeking a living in order to pray for their dead relatives; don Pedro and his wife sell their house to raise money for the dead. Upon his death, don Pedro joins the soul of the corrupt widow's husband, who laments the squandering of his property that should have gone to finance masses to shorten his confinement, and other souls who complain of people's neglect. Don Pedro's widow has little left to spend on her husband's soul, the two of them having expended their resources on other dead, but the priest assures her that she can help him with her prayers and tears. Lorenzo and his wife do gain admittance to heaven, while in the other play Christ promises Mary that he will help don Pedro and his companion souls. The emphasis, in these two plays, on the worthy dead as a focus of attention for the living is a more instructive model than the simple sanctions against greed, lust, and murder. A good person is not simply one who avoids serious sin but one who actively serves the dead. These plays reinforce the cultural attention to the dead introduced into colonial Nahua practice through will-making, confraternities, indulgences, and funerary rites.

Four of the five plays (all except "The Merchant") feature courtroom drama, with Christ sitting in judgment as others testify regarding the moral fitness of the human characters. These scenes vary in regard to who conducts the interrogations and what questions are asked, and more variations are found among the doctrinal texts discussed earlier. Given this variability, people may have formulated quite different notions of how their judgment and sentencing would proceed. However, the general idea that one would appear before Christ and undergo questioning or provide an accounting of oneself may have been widely disseminated. The Nahuatl and Spanish words used for this accounting—*cuenta* in Spanish, words based on *pohua*, "to count," in Nahuatl—support a notion of enumeration, how many good and how many bad things one did, rather than some more abstract testimony of faith.[18] Since, in general, priests had great difficulty eliciting "good" confessions from Nahuas or inducing a fear of hell among them, the idea of the judgment of the soul may not have worked very well as a tool for policing and disciplining the self. Nahuas may have seen it simply as a frightening thing that had to be endured on the way to purgatory, like the obsidian winds and clashing mountains that afflicted their ancestors' *-yolia* en route to the place of the dead.

Nowhere in the dramas is sinful behavior, or the failure of the humans to heed the admonitions of angels, connected explicitly to indigenous identity—it is the people of earth in general who are in this sorry state. There is a universality to these representations of sin and death. And yet, by depicting death and the afterlife in such concrete manners, the plays may actually have reinforced rather than challenged the this-worldly orientation of Nahua religiosity. Hell is described as an abyss and represented theatrically as a substage area or a house. Heaven is revealed behind doors or curtains, and one can climb there on a ladder. When souls leave their bodies they are visible, portrayed by children or other actors. Christ, Mary, demons, and angels appear in visible, concrete form, and so do abstractions such as Death himself, a distinct and morally positive, not evil or fearsome, character. The souls—or, at the world's end, the living people and the resurrected dead—appear before Christ as before a judge at court or a priest at confession. The world after death does not seem like an utterly unknown and immaterial world beyond. This aspect may have helped to make these and similar plays persuasive, if not in substantially changing people's moral attitudes or behaviors, at least in forming their images of their posthumous fate and encouraging people to seek a good death through participation in Christian sacraments, confraternities, prayers, and the making of wills with bequests for masses.

Notes

1. The term *-yolia*, like those referring to other body parts, is obligatorily possessed, always appearing in texts with a possessive prefix, never as an absolutive noun. In this it differs

from the other animating essences, *tonalli*, "heat," "fate," "day," and *ihiyotl*, "breath," which were less tied up with individual identity.

2. This figure may have recalled both the day-sign *miquiztli*, represented by a skull, in the traditional 260-day ritual calendar, and the deity Mictlantecuhtli, or Lord of the Place of the Dead, whom colonial texts sometimes identify with Lucifer but who was represented as a skeleton and was not evil. However, as use of the ritual calendar and memories of preconquest deities lapsed in the colonial era, such connections may have been relevant only for the first generation or so after the conquest, at least in urban areas.

3. All translations are my own unless otherwise noted.

4. Translation by Barry D. Sell and John Frederick Schwaller.

5. In the Mesoamerican vigesimal system, this is an ideal number (twenty counts of twenty) used to represent the idea of a large quantity.

6. One of the Nahua terms applied to sacramental confession, based on a preconquest rite of purificatory confession, was *yolmelahua* or "to straighten (one's or someone's) heart." Another commonly used term was *yolcuitia*, literally "to cause (someone or oneself) to take heart," which I translate as "confess."

7. Josaphat in the text; this placement derives from the Book of Joel (3:2), where this valley is the site of a prophesied final battle between God and his enemies (Stafford Poole, personal communication, 2000).

8. In Matthew 19:28, Jesus tells his disciples that "in the regeneration when the Son of man shall sit in the throne of his glory, ye also shall sit upon twelve thrones, judging the twelve tribes of Israel."

9. This passage recalls the "hellmouth" motif common in medieval art and drama, which represents the entrance into hell as a gaping mouth in the earth.

10. The right and left hands had, respectively, positive and negative associations for Europeans that did not necessarily carry over into the Nahua context. For preconquest Nahuas, the left side, based on the sun's viewpoint when crossing over the sky, was associated with winter (when the sun rose and set toward the south), the dry season, and warfare, but not evil. Indeed, for a ruler to place someone on his left hand was a compliment, as seen in the figure of speech "I will place you on my left, in my obsidian sandals" (Sahagún 1950–1982, 6:259).

11. Text repeats *oannechycnotlaquentique*, "you clothed me with pity," but *oannechycnotlaqualtique* was probably intended.

12. *Tlactli*, the trunk of the body and, by extension, the body as a whole. Use of this term reflects the fact that Nahuatl lacked a term corresponding precisely to *cuerpo*.

13. These examples come from published transcriptions and translations of the wills; I have adapted the translations to my own style.

14. This was, indeed, a point of contention between the regular and the secular clergy; the latter accused the former of laziness for not going out to people's homes to administer this sacrament (Stafford Poole, personal communication, 2000).

15. Neither of these approaches the length of a manual composed for use with Spanish speakers, part of the *Directorio para confesores* issued by the Third Mexican Provincial Council of 1585 (*Directorio del Sancto Concilio Provincial Mexicano celebrado este año de 1585*, MS in Biblioteca Nacional, Madrid; I thank Stafford Poole, C.M., for this information).

16. Vocative suffixes are used but the text could be easily adapted by a female speaker. This prayer is in Burkhart 2001.

17. Spanish-language summaries of indulgences for other confraternities were also published in Mexico. For example, a 1584 publication relating to the confraternity of the Most Holy Sacrament (*Sumario de las Indulgencias*, 1584) enumerates generous indulgences for those who, at certain times or intervals, pray sets of five Our Fathers and one Hail Mary in reverence to that sacrament.

18. Sell's essay (this volume) discusses this usage of the Spanish loan *cuenta*.

NAHUATL CATECHISTIC DRAMA

New Translations, Old Preoccupations

Daniel Mosquera

A few years ago while I was working at the National Archives in Mexico City, a friend—knowing about my interest in Nahuatl drama—inquired why anyone would spend so much time studying it. After all, he insisted, there were histories, treatises, relations, religious doctrine and teachings, and heaps of Nahuatl legal documentation under continuous scrutiny that could be more pertinent to a student of Mesoamerica. His reasoning was based partly on the belief that catechistic drama written and performed in Nahuatl was largely an extension of Spanish devotional and sacramental plays, with an added dimension of "disorientation." He noted that, when judged against Spanish *autos*, *loas*, and *farsas*, Nahuatl drama seemed imperfect and simplistic, and that it could scarcely provide any new substantial information on Nahua contact with Christianity. Although I found his argument uninformed, it left me with the feeling that I had already encountered, partially and in various guises, similar deliberations. This quandary brought to my attention the difficulties in assessing the character of this drama while analyzing the expansion, expression, and performance of Christianity.[1]

There is not a pooled or detailed colonial record, Spanish or Nahua, of the process involved in the overall production of the dramas, although some recent analyses have furnished very valuable findings.[2] How did the dramas arrive in the continent and what use did they receive after arrival? Who was responsible for their adaptation into Nahuatl and what methods were employed? How were the dramas enacted and what kind of affinities developed between neophytes and performances? Who supervised their organization and performances and what concrete effect did they have on the transmission and settlement of Christian doctrine and practices? Did the dramas play a significant social role in the arrangement of popular Christianities and the diffusion of distinctive cults, and did participants affirm any type of Nahua Christian identity?[3] Can devotional and catechistic spectacles and practices in colonial Mexico and medieval and early modern Spain offer insights about each other? In the past twenty years, questions posed by diverse scholars about agencies, especially Nahua agencies, during the first two centuries of Spanish colonization have provoked a general reassessment of the Christianizing campaign. The study of Mesoamerica has much profited from this situation, as more translations of Nahuatl records and discerning scholarship come to fruition. In light of a series of new translations of Nahuatl texts—this volume embodying but one such undertaking—and to the extent that they afford supportive interpretations, I would like to endeavor in this essay a plausible approach to some of the questions contemplated here.

Although Spanish religious drama before the late fifteenth century is to this day still a partial mystery, some observations are feasible by looking at legal documentation, Councils, medieval laws, and city and township records. Clerical culture in New Spain undoubtedly had access to numerous sources of doctrine and biblical lore; *sermonarios* and compilations of *exempla* and *autos* may have often traveled with some of the friars. I will start by examining in a comparative way the historical contexts for Nahuatl catechistic drama, to the degree that they can be localized, and by hazarding some ideas about the intricacies of continuity and transformation tied typically to any act of exchange between cultures. I will then look at each piece individually and in relation to other dramas, especially in connection with the practice of penance and confession, venturing some observations about "radicalized spectacles" that may help us to reevaluate Nahuatl drama.[4]

Catechistic Drama and Popular Culture: A Comparative Analysis

Nahuatl drama reflects a complex interplay of social, religious, and political negotiations between, for the most part, transmissible beliefs and attitudes, some of fascinating adaptability.[5] A similar interplay could be said of Catholicism as it has evolved in many parts of Latin America today. Like most Nahuatl writing, catechistic drama discloses elements that go beyond simple emulation and instruction. Hence, reducing any interpretation of Nahuas under Spanish rule and instruction to a mere trade-off between resistance and conversion is, as James Lockhart has underscored in his work, to miss the mark (1991, 10; 1992, 2–3, 203). In connection to the Nahua, the questions then arise: what of either Spanish or Nahua extraction survives, or "continues," and how has it been shaped by the evolution of religious, social, or political practices? Recent answers to these questions have challenged many of the earlier assumptions, and the methodologies that address the former have emphasized different sources, hence resulting in often contradictory conclusions.[6] This section will be concerned partially with the question, What of Spanish extraction survives? by comparing what characterizes the interaction between popularized and intractable Christian tenets in Spanish and postconquest Nahua settings.

At first sight, this query may seem oversimplifying, even unorthodox, but reaching out to medieval studies may facilitate understanding. If we accept Aron Gurevich's claim that coexisting traditions within Christianity are applicable to medieval Spain, we may begin by asking how New Spain compares. Although circumstances were far from analogous, we might hazard some generalizations. Christianization was administered in both continents to proselytes and followers in different stages using an assortment of tactics, sometimes by force and often by instruction. In Europe, Christianizing forces proved unable to eradicate "folkloric culture" and instead were compelled to interact with it, to the extent that "in both cultures earthly and supernatural, material and spiritual planes merged" (Gurevich 1993, xvi).[7] The popularization of Christian doctrine in Europe inevitably brought the transformation of Christianity, although, Gurevich argues, "in the sphere of hagiography the adjustment of the requirements of theology to the requirements of the masses remained under the Church's control: the legend, the *vita* and the 'miracles,' whatever their folkloric sources may have been, flowed out of the clergy's pen" (1993, 78). The early medieval scriptural tradition to which Gurevich refers comprised penitentials, confession handbooks, and casuistry guides for priests, all of which assisted the Church in dealing with popular traditions "not only about saints, but also in a much wider circle comprising beliefs, perceptions and practices, in order to subordinate these to the demands of official religiosity" (1993, 78).

Colonial Mexico, we must recall, abounded in precisely these types of texts.[8] Addressing the issues of what official religiosity assimilated and how both cultures interacted in this process becomes central to any study of popular religious practices. In reconciling what is "penned" with what is learned, a new problem arises as we then try to gauge what exactly is the result. The example of the story of the Virgin of Guadalupe and the miracles she performed in Mexico seems to have had precisely this sort of trajectory. Although reaching no definitive conclusion about *how* Laso de la Vega's Nahuatl version (*Huei tlamahuiçoltica*) came into being, Sousa et al. illustrate a composite of strategies revealing official and nonofficial mediation throughout. The hypotheses proposed in the preliminary study suggest a compound agency in the production of the text. The sudden late popularity of the cult, the possible manifestation of graphic and textual influences, the probable mediation of Nahua aides, even the possibility of material circulating orally and affecting the outcome and transmission of the story unveil a very intricate scenario (Sousa et al. 1998, 1–47). In a sense, the Christian icon through hagiography becomes a kind of sponge with various performative functions. For the Church the most important of these would be to appropriate the forces comprising "gentile" or pagan religion (Gurevich 1993, 102).

Drawing from his extensive experience with Nahuatl texts and community records, Lockhart presents an argument about Spanish-Nahua interaction that could well be applied to the medieval situation described by Gurevich. Let us consider his ideas at length:

> Change went on constantly, and it occurred precisely because of contact with Spaniards. Increasing degrees of contact with the numerically growing and territorially expanding Hispanic population caused successive general waves of indigenous structural readjustment. The Spaniards represented, however, more the fuel than the motor of the development. They did not, by themselves, either individually or en masse, determine the nature of change; *change was a transaction between two groups and two cultures. . . . it was the nature of Nahua culture in relation to Spanish culture that determined the shape (as opposed to the tempo) of change.* (Lockhart 1992, 21; my emphasis)[9]

Although cognizant of these cultural transactions, the Church did not always ignore this mutual adaptation of cultures, in particular when it dealt with public displays of devotion and religiosity that did not resemble official practices. Both in Europe and

New Spain, there were repeated official attempts to control the proliferation of doctrinal material and its dramatic production in situations that were perceived by the Church as being suspect. In fact, from the beginning the Church was mistrustful of any type of "translation," in general, as became manifest in the various councils that regulated the number of feasts, religious dramas, and the participation of the populace.[10]

Without mentioning religious drama per se or referring specifically to the New World, the Council of Trent (1545–1563) advocated strong regulation of doctrinal and liturgical matters and of their diffusion. This concern prompted, among other Councils, the Council at Salamanca in 1565 to require strict revision of the material used in Nativity plays (demanding local ecclesiastical supervision of performance and texts for approval) and the Council of Toledo to prohibit completely any performance of plays and dances during religious services (Harris 1992, 193). Attempting to solve this problem, the general amendment Urban VIII authored in the Council of 1642 (*Universa per Orbem*) regulated the number and quality of feasts.[11]

In 1555, midway through the Council of Trent, the First Concilio Provincial in Mexico was under way. Here the preoccupation about "translation" was naturally more literal and the overall concern toward the intactness of doctrine more crucial. The first *Capítulo* censures Spaniards and Nahuas alike—the former probably because of the frequent insufficiency of native language knowledge to impart doctrine; the latter because of the belief that Nahuas were by definition inadequate to translate, least of all transmit, complex theological ideas:

> Que no se den a los yndios sermones en su lengua y que ninguna doctrina se traduzga en lengua de indios si no fuere examinada por clérigo o religioso que entienda la lengua en que se traduze.—Muy grandes inconvenientes hallamos que se siguen de dar sermones en la lengua de los indios, así por no entender como por los herrores y faltas que hazen quando los trasladan; por ende statuimos y mandamos que de aquí adelante no se den sermones a los indios para trasladar ni tener en su poder; y los que tienen se les tomen y recojan.

> That no sermons be given to the Indians in their language and no doctrine be translated into Indian languages without being examined by a cleric or friar who knows the language in question.—We have discovered grave mistakes that continue to be preached in Indian languages, either from not understanding or not having translated things well; we require and state by law that from now on no sermon be given to Indians to translate or keep in their power; and if any Indian has any it must be confiscated. (Cited in Llaguno 1962, 167–68).[12]

This passage suggests as well that cleric-inspired sermons may have circulated unsupervised among Nahuas, who in turn utilized them to preach their own understanding of Christianity. This general official unease with the management of religiosity included also the authority to allot divine powers to objects, people, and phenomena, and the access natives had to liturgical ritual objects: "[S]tatuymos y mandamos que se tenga muy gran cuidado por los ministros que no permitan ni consientan que [los indios] traten las cosas sagradas ni que en su poder aya hostias, porque de tenerlas se an seguido escándalos y cosas muy sospechosas . . . por lo cual mandamos a los dichos curas y clérigos que no permitan a los dichos yndios thener en su poder y a su dispusiçion las dichas hostias ni el olio ni crisma" (We order and require that great care be taken by ministers not to allow that [the natives] deal with sacred things nor that they have access to wafers, since, were they to have them, suspicious and scandalous things may occur . . . because of this we order the aforementioned priests and clerics not to allow the Indians to have access to the said wafers nor the consecrated oils; Llaguno 1962, 168). There was continuous anxiety about precisely how the natives were voicing and practicing their Christianity, although no remedy ever contemplated prohibiting dramatic performances altogether.

The provisional synod of 1565 proscribed any written material from the Holy Scriptures from falling into native hands, except for catechisms properly supervised by the prelates (Ricard 1966, 56–57). The Third Concilio Mexicano of 1585 speaks of supervising the use of masks ("máscaras y ynsignias") and controlling dances within the churches, recommending instead that the dances be performed outside: "donde se vea lo que hazen y se pueda oyr y entender lo que cantan; y en los dias de ffiesta no se hagan hasta después de misa mayor por la mañana" (where we may see what they do and hear and understand what they sing; and they are not to do it during feast days until after high Mass in the morning; Llaguno 1962, 286). This Council issued an edict to curb the propagation of profane dances and *representaciones* during religious festivities, demanding that only if they adhered to doctrine and "useful devotion" could they receive authorization from the archbishop at least a month before the performance (García Icazbalceta 1968, 353). Later, in Europe, Urban VIII expressed alarm in 1625, 1631, and 1640 in connection with the unofficial proliferation of hagiographic material, as the Church sought to normalize the rise of miracles, the multiplication of saints, and the like (Rubial García 1997, 56).

The performance of religious plays inside the churches and in public spaces also worried the Church. References dating back to the first Fathers reveal a growing discomfort with dramatic performances in general. From the fifteenth through the eighteenth centuries, ecclesiastical authorities in Europe struggled for control over the use made of sacred material during feasts and celebrations. Spain was no exception. National and provincial Councils in Aranda (1473), Gerona (1475), and Toledo (1565) condemned and censured excesses, "abusos y profanaciones," deriving from more direct participation of the townspeople in religious *representaciones* (Cotarelo 1904, 16).

Medieval Spanish dramas, specifically liturgical and religious drama, are scarce, resulting in a variety of scholarly conjectures about origins and transformations. The often-quoted fourteenth-century *Siete partidas* suggests that there was a drama based on biblical motifs, "que mueven a los homes a facer bien et haber devocion en la fe . . . et demás porque los homes á hayan remembrança que segunt aquello fueron fechas de verdat" (that move men to do good and to be devotedly faithful . . . and besides so that men will remember that they were made of truthful [events]; Cotarelo 1904, 16). What is most remarkable of Alfonso X's law (34, tít. 6, *Partida I*), though not surprising, is that the performances are restricted to the big cities where there are bishops and archbishops who can supervise them: "et non lo deben facer en las aldeas, nin en los lugares viles, nin por ganar dineros con ello" (and they must not be performed in villages, nor vile places, nor for profit; 16). Stern has suggested that given the

Church's endorsement of Nativity and Easter plays in the document, such dramas must have been known at least in Castile (1996, 76).

Echoing Gurevich's analysis of the penitentials in the early Middle Ages, Stern offers an assessment that resonates with views of Nahuatl drama as interpreted in this essay. She contends that official Latin writings treated the relationship between pre-Christian and Christian worldviews as sequential, whereas the Latin hagiographies, visions of the otherworld, and penitentials validated the belief that Christianity had assimilated much of the pre-Christian world: "Thus the two cultures coexisted and interacted in complex and contradictory ways" (Stern 1996, 72).

Although just over two centuries after the believed performance of "Final Judgment" in Tlatelolco, a case dating to 1768 and investigated by the Inquisition in Mexico seems to present a telling example of this type of situation. News came to the Holy Office that in the town of Ozumba, parish of Tlalmanalco, a play representing the Passion of Christ "en disposición cómica" (in a comical fashion) was presented annually on Easter Sunday. The documents allege that the performance of the play included an irreverent Judas and a naked native Christ who also consecrated the Host during the Last Supper:

> y saliendo al teatro el que hace el papel de Jesucristo desnudo públicamente con grande indecencia y escándalo con la gravísima circunstancia de que cuando se hace la Cena simula éste que consagra y alza una hostia y se hincan todos a adorarla; y finalmente, que a todo esto preceden los ensayos que para su ejecución se hacen y empiezan desde mediada la Cuaresma, los que se ejecutan de noche, convidando la gente para que asista a son de caja, que salen tocando por las calles y plaza desde la oración hasta las nueve de la noche, que dan principio al ensayo, el que se finaliza a más de la medianoche.[13]

> and appearing in the play (is) the one who plays Jesus, naked in public and with great indecency and scandal, adding the grave circumstance that when they enact the Last Supper he simulates the consecration, raising a wafer, after which everyone kneels to praise it; and finally that all of this is preceded by rehearsals done at night which start from mid-Lent, inviting the people to come using drums, which they play in the streets and plazas from the Prayer until nine o'clock when they start the rehearsal, ending past midnight.

A *Comisario*, notary, and priest were assigned to this and other locations in the province of Chalco to look into the allegations, resulting in over a hundred folios. The legal process included interrogations of members of the community who had played different roles over the years and the subsequent confiscation of plays written in Spanish and Nahuatl. The copies that were confiscated probably represented similar versions of the text of the Passion cycle.

This may not have been an isolated case, however. Nahuas had organized their own confraternities since the sixteenth century, starting in the bishopric of Mexico with the confraternity of Santiago in Tlatelolco, Veracruz in Xochimilco, and Santo Cristo de Burgos in Culhuacan (Bazarte Martínez 1989, 46). Confraternities soon multiplied in the seventeenth century with natives joining in with Spaniards ("cofradías mixtas" such as Santísimo Sacramento and Ánimas Benditas) or forming their own assemblies. The confraternities in Mexico had a cohesive influence on the preservation of communities, but, most important, they offered a platform on which the community itself could protect and hoist its own cults. "Su objeto principal, a pesar de los curas y párrocos, no fue la difusión del catolicismo sino la fiesta del santo patrón" (their main objective, in spite of priests and friars, was not the dissemination of Catholicism but the feast of the patron saint; Bazarte Martínez 1989, 44). There is abundant documentation that reveals much activity with *retablos* and *representaciones* made for festivities related to sanctioned cults; other attempts were persecuted or penalized, though the plays in question are not mentioned. For instance, one Juan Rivera from Tepecoacuilco was summoned, to be later absolved, for having presented a *comedia* to the Indians of Tuxpan in the presbytery of the church.[14] Although there is no description of the type of play, it is likely that it had some religious content. The province of Chalco represents one among many examples that has auspiciously been documented, in which ecclesiastical authorities tried to control the circulation of popular religious devotion.

The Dramas

Described often by the friars as a persecutory mobilization against the devil, the Christianizing campaign had a very concrete effect on the social life of the natives. A massive and expanding campaign was deployed, staging a series of instructional negotiations that served, in different degrees, to establish a Christian presence in New Spain without eradicating local traditions and beliefs. As has been noted by historians of early America, this was a double-edged attempt. On the one hand, the early friars sought to understand better the very customs they wanted to eradicate. On the other hand, they modeled a frequently erratic catechization on those documented Nahua beliefs.

Among the various strategies of Christian didacticism, catechistic drama stood out and was very instrumental in attracting Nahuas to Christian practices, at least initially those drawn more by spectacle and festivity. We can surmise that among the main didactic goals was to transport the natives back to a mythical origin, in this case biblical, the backdrop against which social, moral, and sacramental notions were implemented. I locate catechistic drama in New Spain in a period of intense religious induction, unparalleled in the history of religious campaigns. If early chronicles are nearly accurate, in New Spain catechistic drama spills over into other territories of everyday life. It is echoed in daily doctrine, narrated in stories and histories, and reenacted constantly in sacramental practices. This analysis examines catechistic drama in the context of cultural and religious transformation. While looking at Nahuatl dramas that promoted specific ideas, I also engage native and Christian notions of recollection, penance, exemplarity, and eschatology.

In a letter dated November 17, 1532, and directed to the King Charles V of Spain, fray Martín de Valencia (1474–1534) describes in succinct and poignant words the extent of the friars' involvement in the religious matters of the indigenous peoples. This Franciscan led the spiritual expedition of the first twelve missionaries arriving in Mexico in 1524 at the behest of Hernando Cortés: "y una de las cosas por donde se conoçe que a nuestro gran Dios le plega que esta nación se salbe, es *averles mostrado el castigo por la ofensa pasada, y darles remedio para escapar de la que obieran incurrido* (and one of the ways whereby we know that God is hopeful for this nation to be saved, is *having shown them (the natives) the punishment of their past offenses and giving them remedy to escape from what they would have done*; Cartas de Indias 1980, 1:54; my emphasis).

A complaint about various judicial and territorial injustices of many of the Spanish colonizers, most of whom participated in the *encomienda* system, this letter is also a summary of some of the processes of transculturation and religious instruction to which the natives were subjected. In this letter, fray Martín refers not only to the former belligerent behavior of some of the Indians (the revolt against Cortés's advances; the constant threat of the Chichimecas, for example) but also to the counteracting attitudes of a good number of elders and *caciques* in the different communities. These beliefs may simply be echoes of the skepticism with which the Nahua leaders were said to have met the twelve Franciscans and their doctrine in 1524.[15] To this scenario is added the quick decimation of the indigenous populations owing to epidemics, which lasted well into the late sixteenth century, overwork, and taxation. The deployment of catechistic drama in the sixteenth and seventeenth centuries meets native responses to Christianization precisely in this crossroads between disinclination and devotion.

"How to Live on Earth" is a drama with many preconquest overtones (Horcasitas 1974, 53).[16] It is a moral and didactic piece with several fictional characters whose good or bad behavior is addressed in terms of restitution. Directed at "all sinners," the drama begins with a calling to those who will honor and serve Jesus:

> God's beloved mother places before us her sadness. Reverently, humbly she places before us her sadness, her weeping swoon. But as for us, we just waste her precious and honored tears, which here on earth lie flowing on account of our sins. And likewise here on earth the precious blood of our beloved honored savior, our lord Christ, has been wasted. Today he gives and shows to all of us sinners his precious and honored passion (11r–v).[17]

"How to Live on Earth" stands out for its insistence on the admission of sin and the need for timely repentance. This insistence is placed at the beginning of the drama, when the newly wed and Christianized Lorenzo voices his concern about how he and his wife will live on earth and whether it is wise, in God's eyes, to seek wealth and personal property (12r). This may be consonant with *contemptus mundi* beliefs exemplified and much emphasized by the early Franciscans. The transactional nature of purgatory as represented during the Middle Ages becomes apparent in this first exchange, as Lorenzo expresses distress about "debt" related to his dead parents and the mediating influence of the Virgin Mary: "Do they owe something to someone here on earth? If only we had for their sake repaid the goods, the silver and gold, precious things, jades, for here on earth they come to an end" (12r–v). Associated not only with material debts inherited from the parents, this bond verbalizes as well a debt to interceding divinities.

First Angel lays emphasis on perseverance and honoring a bond ("a precious cord of heaven") that is vulnerable to the deceptions of the *tzitzimitl* (12v; see below for a discussion of this term), whereas a rather eloquent First Demon identifies the negation of Christian rites as his locus of action (13r–v). In fact, much of what is demanded from the characters stresses a proper exchange in which listening plays a major role and much is submitted to judgment, both divine and demonic. Praying for the dead before God and the Virgin becomes initially a point of contention between Angel and First Demon. The demon, by placing emphasis on inappropriate Christian behavior, defines his world of action in terms of dissidence and deviation, revealing an interesting strategy. This economics of penance in which the living help the dead—and them-selves by atoning for the latter—may teach Christian contempt toward the accumula-tion of material goods and their obsolescence in God's kingdom, but it also directs attention to valuations of debt. Deliverance is presented then in the context of a tribu-tary religious and social affiliation. The subsequent appearance of a mother scolding a child concentrates on obedience and going to church, although the general theme of praying for others remains pivotal.

This affiliation through penance also signals an apprehension over Christian ret-ributive rites, announcing a type of reckoning that graduates the "new economy" in a scale of transactional values (such as gold and silver, property, debt, and so on), all or part of which will level off with continuous prayer and remembrance. It is a reminder and reenactment of a bondage whose symbolic power may effect radical change. The verbal clash of demons and angels—the latter of which continually, according to First Demon, rob him of his servants—addresses this possibility as well. The drama calls attention to valuations of indigenous reality in connection to Christian penitential and retributive observances, emphasizing vassalage and subjugation to diametrically opposed forces: to devils and to God. A double effect is conceivable, in terms of the series of expectations produced by angels and devils, since both had the role of por-traying for the audience specific behavioral examples while, at the same time, eliciting fear.

In a way, the drama was directing attention to the preconquest reluctance to con-fess sins immediately after they happen, waiting instead until the moment of death. We know that the natives considered confession a final option, expecting absolution and clearance from the law for crimes such as adultery or for other transgressions (Soustelle 1955, 234–35). In "How to Live on Earth," early confession is rewarded, as First Angel proclaims to the devil, stressing the need for recollection: "You declare that they do not cry out to me, that they do not remember me" (13r). During this exchange, First Demon recalls the original sin by offering a short summary of the Fall (15r), an event that should evoke specific images to a Nahua audience that had been exposed to Christian doctrine for several decades. As in medieval drama, maintaining interconnectedness among the various plays and themes was an important feature here made more significant by the reminder of what was probably one of the earliest Nahuatl plays.[18] The play is in any case inhabited by references to remembrance and accounting, repayment, retribution, and confession, in connection with the living and the dead.

Other characters appear in the drama, including several in their formative years. They exemplify choices that reflect similar concerns over proper observances such as confession (17v–18v). In the character's final reckoning, several "souls" approach the dying one, Lorenzo, as the heavenly gates open. This episode is followed by insistent petitions on the part of these helping souls "to repay [Lorenzo and his wife's] love," to repay the sadness and pity they endured, and in turn to pray for those who will soon join God (25v). In a drastic change of scenes accompanied by trumpets, a Christ figure imparts judgment as he reminds the Virgin about her sufferings and his final torment (26v–27r); again, this is reminiscent of other biblical passages the audience had probably seen enacted before. The final moments contain as much violence as can be expected of any medieval play related to the Final Judgment, as orders direct the demons to hang, beat, and tear to pieces the disrespectful one. Condemned leaves, crying to the spectators, "You who bring up children, you who raise children, do not be idiotic, as if you were not rational. Open your ears! Listen to the sermon and the exemplary model. You are not going to fall into the fiery crag like I am now about to do!" (28v). The moral illustration of this drama is intensified by the violence of the final scene.

In an excellent study on medieval drama and violence, Jody Enders has concluded that there is a strong connection, inherited from the classical rhetorical era, between torture and truth. Showing that "the medieval understanding of torture both enabled and encouraged the dramatic representation of violence as a means of coercing theater audiences into accepting the various 'truths' enacted didactically in mysteries, miracles, and even farces" (1999, 2–4), Enders concludes that much of this cruelty was, and continues to be, fundamental to rhetoric (232). We may not deem as fully reliable Motolinia's and others' enthusiastic descriptions of natives' participation in Nahuatl dramas, but we can surmise a remarkable growing devotion that owed as much to the language's ability to transmit powerful emotions as to the natives' adherence to signs that verified some sense of continuity.

The friars' recurring insistence on the natives' pre-Christianity may, therefore, have had a wider application than has been documented in the dramas. It not only infiltrated the religious fabric of the community but also instituted a consciousness of restitution for a series of offenses perhaps unknown until then. When the act of atonement for a newly defined "sin" then becomes public—for example, renunciation of idolatrous customs, various penitential and retributive offerings—the whole community participates in this act and is thus subjected to a new chain of events. Catechistic drama epitomizes the most elaborate link in this chain, since it serves the purpose of both instituting a presumed new order and inviting collective participation in its transmission.

Even so, the practice and ritualization of confession were not foreign to the Mesoamerican experience but are, in fact, among the many similarities between Nahua and Christian religions that were noted and documented, with distinct ideological intentions, by several of the early chroniclers. Striking in one of Las Casas's descriptions of this practice is his observation of native inclination to extreme dramatism when carrying out penitential acts. These were done, according to Las Casas, for reasons of a mythical-cosmic value or because a transgression had been recognized by them. In several ways, this capacity in the natives for doing penance, in the context of Christian purgatorial rites, had profound implications. Las Casas further explains:

> todos guardaban inviolablemente aquestas cerimonias, porque allende que si se sabía que alguno algo dellas quebrantaba, era ásperamente castigado, tenían vehementísimo temor que de cierto habían en breve de morir, según estimaban

ser gravísimo ese pecado, y sábese por los nuestros religiosos que comúnmente acaecía así, o porque el demonio (permitiéndolo Dios), les causaba la muerte con obras que para ello hacía, para tenellos más devotos y ligados en aquella penitencia y cerimonias de su servicio, o porque *la imaginación de haber cometido pecado que tenían por tan grave, solía ser tan vehemente que de pura tristeza se morían.* (1967, 2:215; my emphasis)

All of them kept to these ceremonies inviolably, because if any part were to be broken, the person would be severely punished, producing such terrible fear that they anticipated death on the spot, if the sin was estimated to be very serious, commonly known by our clergy to be the case, or because the Devil (God permitting), caused them to die, in order to instill in them more devotion and to keep them fastened to penitence and rites to his service, or because *the thought of having committed a sin they considered to be terrible was so vehement that they would die of sadness.*

This dynamic of guilt becomes, in fact, a conditioning factor almost in a psychosomatic way: the ritual of retribution finds expression through the suffering of the body.

In addition, doing penance is described both as an act of contrition and regret and as a fundamental part of many sacrificial rites; yet, what is most significant in Las Casas's description is the identification of the natives' capacity to acquire a consciousness of guilt through an act of re-creation ("la imaginación de haber cometido pecado" [the imagination of having committed a sin]). In the context of New Spain's incipient Christianity, this retribution also may have acquired material and spiritual value and was much exploited in catechistic drama in the attempt to infuse an ideology of continence and retribution. The drama exploited this disposition in the natives by emphasizing the anguish of mental and spiritual distress that medieval drama exploited so consistently.

Through the verbal act of penitence and confession the individual becomes, in a personal and social sense, confronted with, and often divorced from, portions of his past.[19] The drama moves from the genesis of the defiled individual (the First Fall, for example, or the institution of sacramental religion) to the representation of a dislodgment patent in the suffering of the body. "Yn Pochtecatl" ("The Merchant"), another Nahuatl drama centered on timely repentance and proper management of goods, presents the suffering of the body as the result of a transgression that translates into a specific sin.[20]

"The Merchant" represents a continuation of the medieval religious drama that instructed by dramatizing didactic narratives. These constructions would concentrate, primarily, on a single occurrence traversing in a linear fashion: from the acting out of a particular experience of sin or transgression to the moment of judgment or retribution, which would end in either salvation or damnation. "Everyman" and "Mankind" are good medieval examples—both morality plays in which a collective humankind, the principal character, is ultimately saved from damnation by personified Christian abstractions such as Good Deeds and Mercy.[21] Although proper and honest deeds are apparent throughout this play, "The Merchant" lacks the allegorized elements of such morality plays, focusing instead on the torments of perdition and the inability to receive timely forgiveness through either repentance or retribution.[22]

"The Merchant" reflects, moreover, Franciscan and Nahua preoccupations about the restitution of goods and timely repentance. The drama has a simple plot, and its main character could be seen as an extension of the Herodian figure, a medieval example of great pride, blindness, and greed. The first words spoken by Merchant at the very beginning of the Nahuatl drama certainly exemplify this view: "No one can equal me in all my power, in all my goods and property, the gold and silver, the jades and emeralds, the precious pearls. No one can equal me in all the diverse precious things that are my pleasures" (44v).[23] "The Merchant" begins with a prologue announcing the character of the drama. It is about a moneylender who did not return the wealth and property taken from others, oppressing others with his dealings, "what happened to his body and his soul was very frightening and very terrifying" (44r). The drama follows a series of encounters between Merchant and several stock figures, dramatizing Merchant's disrespect toward doing penance and his fall into the sins of avarice and "cobdicia." The play ends by expressing concern about spiritual regeneration, implied in Christian salvation.

The emphasis on the refusal to grant mercy even after penitential conditions are met introduces a stringent view of redemption. Bevington recognizes, concerning medieval morality plays, that placing emphasis on penitential scourging and good deeds as the only means to salvation may have had to do with the assumption of "some urgency in the context of the late fifteenth century, when abuses among the clergy and disaffection among worshippers were on the increase" (1975, 939). In sixteenth- and seventeenth-century Mexico, disaffection among worshippers may have provided this tone and context. Without losing sight of the dogma of salvation, "The Merchant" transforms these concerns into instruments of fear. The specific sin around which this drama is constructed is usury, and the context in which this sin is dramatized suggests the existence of tributary relationships in which Merchant exerts control over Notary and Alcalde, and "weak-minded" women and men of various ages.[24] From the early ideographic prayers and primers to doctrines, sermon books, and confessionaries, catechistic and instructional material dealt with the Christian dogma of sins, some of which may have invited performances.[25] Predictably, the evangelizing campaign had at its disposal a wide range of dramatic images to reassert continuously paradigms of exemplarity and suffering. The sin around which this play is built may speak to Spanish preoccupations about native behavior and may address possible Nahua unease over Spanish abuse of authority.

Merchant's continual breaking of the Ten Commandments and the Commandments of the Church is accompanied by repeated references to bodily pain and punishment, threats of dismemberment, imprisonment, and torture.[26] The most revealing episode related to this last point occurs when Merchant demands Notary's help to forge some documents in order to procure a woman's property and money (48r–v). The woman is a widowed mother, whose husband had left his wealth and property for Merchant to keep (47v). Merchant is summoned as soon as the complaint reaches the judge. When he appears in court he swears in vain, breaking the First Commandment. Priest then reminds Merchant of the futility of accumulating material goods: "know that when you die you will not take any of your goods and property with you . . . help yourself [for] no one else can help you" (49v–50r). This exchange between Mother, Merchant, and

Priest includes the flouting of a specific Christian law framed by the dispossession of material goods, as God's kingdom comes nearer.

Strikingly relevant, and indicative that this drama may have addressed Spaniards as well as natives, is that the play was perhaps attending to a growing problem in Nahua communities, that of land titles and inheritance, as has become evident in much of the work done on testaments, wills, and other legal documents. As Spaniards' and *criollos*' numbers increased, Nahua communities saw their lands diminish and conflicts increase regarding property that was inherited (or not). Many of the testaments attest to pervasive confusion and dishonesty, as the different communities responded to changes imposed by Spanish officialdom, many of which reassigned political value to rulers and communities (see Lockhart 1992, 28–47). The impositions served to advance Nahua as much as Spanish geopolitical organizations.

When the demons make an entrance, the sick man recognizes himself as a defiled body: "My soul is about to perish and my earthly body is very mired down" (51v). The struggle that ensues between forces of angels and demons is both a summons to confess and a calling to renounce association with the devil and a life of sin. The priest stresses precisely this need, as he advises the now too-late repentant sick man: "[God] wants you to save yourself so that you merit and attain his royal home, for you are likely to die when you least expect it. And now he concedes to you time to save yourself by confessing" (52r). At the end, Merchant is made the victim of terrible suffering in hell. He endures further pain at the hands of devils—they choke him to death. His death and the departure of his soul are represented with the "blackened soul" and the sound of rockets. It appears that the Mexicans had grown very fond of pyrotechnic elements used in the dramas, and fireworks served also to announce the fall into hell by one of the boys in "How to Live on Earth" (Horcasitas 1974, 127). The sound effects may have echoed preconquest ones. The sight of the tormented body as the character is led to the place of the dead *(mictlan)*, in the midst of pyrotechnic sounds, must have certainly generated amusement and perhaps fear. It still remains a mystery how color played a part in such effects.

The enigmatic ending of "The Merchant" is accompanied by the words of Guardian Angel. It is a warning to prevent the community going astray from the righteous path of a presumably rediscovered Christian life. The words are also a reminder of the loss of a Judeo-Christian link in the distant, biblical past. The drama, however, makes manifest a strong correlation between the human and the social body in terms of acknowledging—through the drama and in a very real sense before Nahua and maybe Spanish authorities—participation in a defiled polity.

Religious allegiance and realignment entrenches itself in the individual and communal performance of guilt. Guilt is also elicited in the context and symbolism of payment and transaction. As Friedrich Nietzsche suggested more than a century ago, there is a close relationship between guilt and pain, both of which occur in the sphere of contracts, debt, and legal obligations (1956, 194–95).[27] It is for this reason that the language of pledge and compensation is frequently present in catechistic dramas.

The drama "Yn Animastin Yhuan Alvaceasme" ("Souls and Testamentary Executors") shares with "The Merchant" the enactment of a final reckoning in terms of payment, debt, and expressions of allegiance. In addition, confession appears as the opening toward the reconciliation of that debt. The staging of several of the dramas such as "The Merchant," "Souls and Testamentary Executors," and "Final Judgment"—all of which included hells and fiery scenes—identified fever and sickness as divine responses to sin and lack of proper penance. Physical experiences of thirst, fire, and dryness came to be associated with fire and condemnation, evident in this example from "The Merchant":

> If your lips are so dry with just a little illness, if you are so thirsty, how can you suffer the fires of hell and the dried cracking of lips in hell which have no other cure? They will make you drink molten lava, which is very hot, very painful and very heart-rending. (52v–53r)

Thirst is well known in Christian tradition as a metaphor, particularly among the mystics, for the need for (and receptivity to) Christian love (agape). In this drama, sickness and the dualities of dryness and wetness, of hot and cold, may have addressed Nahua as much as Christian cosmic values. Ortiz de Montellano (1990, 8) and López Austin (1988, 380–85) noted that the natives treated disease completely on a supernatural plane; that is, on a plane that was in accord with the animistic view of the universe. López Austin further asserts that the supernatural "was judged to be material, potentially visible, tangible, and audible" (1988, 383). So there was a causal connection between the different planes of the gods and the earth. The friars capital-ized on the coincidence of sickness and native religious beliefs, attempting to equate one with the other and attributing both to divine retributive intervention.

According to Christian Duverger, the expression of these dualities in penitential acts was related to the Nahua *tonalli* (1978, 184). The *tonalli* was connected with the maintenance of balance, in particular if it included penitential offerings (184). In other words, the offering of blood (bloodletting) created a direct link, inscribed in the individual since the moment of birth, between the individual and the divinity; the offering's sole purpose was the sustenance and continuance of a cosmic order that gave the community its balance (184–85). In the eyes of the clergy, this manifestation of the natives' need to maintain a cosmic balance through suffering and chastisement became an indication of a certain messianic symbolism. Catechistic representations of penance documented and employed this symbolism in the guise of accountability.

The beginning of "Souls and Testamentary Executors" illustrates this inclination.[28] Don Pedro, one of the central characters, speaks to his wife of his distress over the dead: "I go about discontent before God concerning the unfortunate dead people. They have already given an accounting to him, already been examined before him concerning their deeds, the various sins, and already been judged" (36v–37r). This drama exhibits an infernal setting that emphasizes the horrors of suffering and pain in the context of demon-affiliation. Lucifer's introductory speech and complaint to the five demons addresses issues of property and payment (or the lack thereof): "Do not uselessly lose it through neglect; really go after those in whose hands the dead left themselves. Go, induce them to dissipate absolutely all the property of the dead so that the souls they are to take from us will not escape from our hands" (38r).

Evidently, the sense is that salvation is at stake for those in purgatory and for those involved in the spectacle of retribution. Recalling the Commandments and remembering the dead also play prominent roles in the play.[29] There is repeated emphasis on dismemberment and torture. At the sound of fireworks, the second executor declares why he is condemned, as he responds to the first executor's cry of despair, "Woe to us who are sinners!" The second executor counters, "It is your fault that we are punished and made to suffer here for I said to you that the goods and property of the souls with which they will be helped should be entered into the church. That is why these things are happening to us now" (47v). Material goods become tangible in the context of retributive cleansing and sin, with clear litigating implications regarding property, its loss and possible recovery.[30]

Confession and the dislodgment of material goods was a transactional phenomenon documented in Motolinia's *Memoriales* (written roughly between 1527 and 1541), where we find extensive descriptions of the presumed results of confession. Motolinia dedicates eight chapters to this sacrament, three of which emphasize the aspect of material retribution. According to Motolinia the practice of the Christian sacrament of penitence started in 1526 (1996, 243). He also pays special attention to the docility and devotion manifest in the natives' approach to Christian confession and penance (243–67). Of particular importance are chapter 32 ("Como los yndios rrestituyen lo que son a cargo porque no se les niegue la absoluçión e vn enxemplo a éste proposito" [How the Indians make restitution of what they have in order to gain absolution and an example concerning this]), and chapter 35 ("Como dan libertad a sus esclauos e rrestituyen lo que no poseen con buen título" [How they free their servants or make restitution of what they do not own through good title]). Both chapters present descriptions of material restitution and specific, short, exempla-like narratives that not only serve as possible testimony of Nahua penitential behavior under colonial rule but also provide us with invaluable anecdotal information about commingling patterns of retribution and penance in sixteenth-century Mexico.

Sahagún describes a penitent Indian in connection with the penance dictated by a Nahua priest or mediator *(tlapouhqui)* (1990, 1:20). When he had finished, the priest imposed on the man a penance that would vary in severity: short or lengthy fasts, scarification of the tongue (which might be pierced through and have as many as eight hundred thorns or straws pushed through the wound), sacrifices to *tlazolteotl*, and various other austerities. Once the man did penance, he could no longer be punished upon this earth (1:20–21). This schema of retribution may find a parallel enactment in the catechistic dramas mentioned in this chapter. Perhaps the most salient characteristic is the repeated voicing of regret and admission of guilt. This admission becomes tangible in the context of Christian salvation or damnation. The last words of Widow in "Souls and Testamentary Executors" attest to this:

> Oh! Oh! Oh! You who will have fasting garments, mourning clothes, do not regard them as frivolous for you are ordered to it through penance, prayers and fasting, and communion will be taken each month. I did not do this and now I am paying the penalty. Let everyone take an example from me. (52r)

She and the executors are carried off to hell by demons in the midst of violent cries and threats of dismemberment. "You who are the house of hell, swallow us up once and for all," cries the second executor. "Let us not look at you [the condemned]. As for you devils, just rip us to shreds once and for all" (52r). This "exemplary sign" or *neixcuitilli* takes the form of a public confession that calls for collective repentance and emulation. In addition, this calling also attempts to generate a consciousness of debt, a radically distinct emphasis from that of preconquest restitution of cosmic order. Sins were not believed to be inherent and could assume independence from the individual, in a metaphorical sense.

Catechistic drama may have had a stronger effect on an audience in the context of broadening the scope of the sin to include, for instance, all those whose "consciousness" of transgression had not yet matured to produce a proper Christian penitential act. Two good examples are "Souls and Testamentary Executors," in which honoring the dead demands constant prayers and vicarious acts of negotiation, and "The Merchant," in which material goods are to be "given back" in time to achieve salvation. In these two cases, salvation does not materialize for the main characters, whose penitential acts of contrition have been either too late in coming or substantially insufficient. The "debt" incurred by the transgression has overridden any supernatural intervention other than that of the devils, all of whom have been reduced in these dramas to inflictors of pain and torture or to mere agents provocateurs with no voice in the legislating process.

This depiction of devils is by no means distant from European models. Much medieval and early modern iconography has devils continuously pestering good and erratic Christians, as becomes evident especially in *exempla*. In New Spain, devils (translated into Nahuatl sometimes as *tzitzimitl* [pl. *tzitzimime*], but most often as *tlacatecolotl* [pl. *tlatlacatecolo*]) seem to be limited generally to vicarious assistants who inflict or threaten to inflict bodily pain and suffering after the Last Judgment or after death. As is to be expected, there were testimonies against the friars and their teachings using terms similar to the ones the friars used to portray devils present among Nahua communities.

A significant example of this is the case of a native called Martin Ucelo (Ocelotl). Evidence in Sahagún and in Inquisition records shows that Ucelo, after more than a decade of exposure to Christian ideas and to preaching, had begun to use his knowledge of these ideas to discredit Christian indoctrination to his own advantage. Residents of Tecalco who knew Ucelo report that he preached against the friars, using doctrinal ideas pertaining to the end of the world. Ucelo refers to the messengers of punishment who will cause destruction (León-Portilla 1974: 26; *Procesos de indios idólatras y hechiceros* 1912, 19–21). Ucelo is reported to have said that the friars would descend turned into "chichimicle" (cf. *tzitzimime*): "si no se pudiese sacar lumbre, que habría fin el linaje humano, y que aquella noche y aquellas tinieblas serían perpetuas . . . y que de arriba vendrían y descenderían los *tzitzimime*, que eran unas figuras feísimas y terribles y que comerían a los hombres y mujeres" (if no fire could be drawn, then there would be the end of the human race, and that the night and darkness would be perpetual . . . and *tzitzimime* would descend, creatures that were very ugly and terrible and would eat humans, men and women; cited in León-Portilla 1974, 27).

Ucelo's imprecations directed attention to the grim nature of Christian eschatology that was manifest in the practices and teachings of the friars. The residents of Tecalco declared that Ucelo had said that "esta ley de los [crist]ianos, no sabéis que nacimos para morir, é que después de muertos no hemos de tener placer ni regocijo; pues por qué no nos folgaremos mientras vivimos" (this Christian law, you do not know we were born to die, and after death we will have no joy nor pleasure; so why not take advantage while we live; *Procesos de indios idólatras* 1912, 27). León-Portilla comments on this same passage, noting that Nahua critiques of the friars recognized, in spite of apparent similarities, a certain absurdity in Christian teachings (1974, 27), which reminds us of similar descriptions found in Muñoz Camargo.[31]

Burkhart describes Nahua fatalism as a felicitous discovery by the friars as they promoted Christian doctrine (1989, 79). The Nahua lacked any notion of punishment after death but they believed that human actions could be responsible for a final destruction, and Burkhart argues that the friars may have found it more effective to associate punishment for sin with the end of the world rather than with individual death (79). This method, she argues, could have coincided more with Nahua views of collectivity and may have deemphasized individual salvation (79); yet salvation was still central in the instructional process that came to be epitomized by the Last Judgment, and several plays ended with raucous and violent renditions of it.

"Nexcuitilmachiotl. motenehua juiçio final" ("Final Judgment") has been hailed as one of the most distinctive of the surviving Nahuatl dramas, with as yet no direct European referent (Horcasitas 1974, 567). It dramatized at a collective level an elaborate and complex event around which much Christian doctrine was erected. The drama represented a heightened convergence of past, present, and future times. In other words, a temporal origin partakes of the collapse of history as we know it, tracing the biblical timeline from the Adamic myth of exile, the Augustinian *felix culpa* of much medieval thought, to the re-alignment of the Last Judgment in which God would mete out punishment or salvation for the living and the dead, including those in purgatory. This judicial event of converging times reenacts therefore a dramatic sequence of recollection. In a very concrete sense, the Last Judgment is centered on acts of remembrance.

Like Motolinia's plagues in his *Historia de los Indios de la Nueva España*, "Final Judgment" is part of European and New World eschatology, a mode of experience and interpretation that anticipates or references the end of times.[32] In both cases, an act of chastening confirms the power of a divinity, reestablishes a causal relationship between states of defilement and cleansing, and tempers any future transgression by promising salvation. In Spain, for example, the theme of divine judgment and redemption enjoyed much popularity, showing a long and varied trajectory. The judgment of humankind and the harrowing of hell were, if not central to, at least ingredients of several Spanish *autos*. Examples of this eschatological drama are the plays "Aucto de la redención del género humano" (Play about the redemption of mankind) and "Aucto de la acusación contra el género humano" (Play about the accusation made against mankind; Rouanet 1979, 2:449, 4:47).[33] For a medieval audience, the moment of the Final Judgment demanded self-examination and connected eschatological readings with the liturgy of Advent and its penitential practices (Bevington 1975, 2). The idea of a Second Advent played a significant role in much of the Franciscan campaign of evangelization, especially in their adaptation of Christian eschatology to Nahua indoctrination.

The mapping of eschatological signs, we have come to realize, had idiosyncratic ritual manifestations in Nahua and Christian cultures. The friars paid close attention to Nahua fatalism and were often quick to draw parallels that accentuated Christian eschatology (Burkhart 1989, 77, 79). Muñoz Camargo explains how God, as a gesture of mercy to the natives, fought the devil and rectified the signs he had truncated and used to mislead the natives by sending new signs along with messengers (1986, 179). The friars equally acknowledged other coincident structures and events.[34] In the context of varied eschatologies, "Final Judgment" is a catechistic drama that represents and promotes more than a simple sacramental sensibility. It reproduces the Christian inferno, acknowledging Nahua fatalism and practices concerning death, yet insisting on specific Catholic practices sanctioned in *doctrinas* and sermons.[35] New Testament condemnation meets indigenous responses to calamity and tribulation.[36]

The drama incorporates a total of seventeen characters that deliver lines, including personified abstractions distinctive of medieval miracle and morality plays, in order of appearance: Saint Michael, Penance, Time, Holy Church, Death, Lucía, Priest, Antichrist, First Living Person, Christ, First Angel, Second Angel, First Dead Person, Second Dead Person, Second Living Person, Third Dead Person, Second Demon, Satan, First Demon, and the Condemned. The structure of the drama follows a linear trajectory, divided into sections that dramatize different exchanges of the Last Judgment.

The Christian theme of the drama belongs to the New Testament, Luke 21:25–33 and Matthew 25:31–46 (Horcasitas 1974, 567), although the theme of rewarding people according to their past behavior populates the Old Testament, apocryphal texts, and all sorts of divinatory lore. In Matthew, we find a reference to the Second Coming, the reenactment of judgment, and the subsequent congregation of living and dead before Christ and his retinue of angels. Luke speaks of a judgment day when the Son of Man will be revealed. Horcasitas speculates that the drama was performed with a general mass (567).

Although the episode of the Antichrist echoes John's Apocalypse, as Horcasitas explains, there is no direct European antecedent to the Nahuatl drama (1974, 567). He cites, as a possible partial source to the Nahuatl Antichrist, the twelfth-century German *Antichristus*, a drama that apparently used also a great number of actors or participants (567). Horcasitas is probably referring to the *Ludus de Antichristo*, the "Play of Antichrist," which McGinn describes as worthy of a Hollywood production because of its immense cast and grand subject matter (1994, 134). In this play, paganism (Gentilitas) and Judaism (Synagoga) enter into dispute with the Christian Church over political and spiritual control of the world, with the subsequent victory of the German emperor, who then fulfills his "apocalyptic function by laying down his crown in Jerusalem" (134). The second and last parts of the play deal with the entrance of the Antichrist, accompanied by Hypocrisy and Heresy; his investiture as false king; and a final refutation that prompts the conversion of the Jews and the collapse of the Antichrist. As with several other Antichrist figures throughout history, he is here identified with theological and political dissent and reformation. Insofar as the Antichrist was considered an evil principle in constant war with Christ, his appearance or fancied personification evoked the end of time and the liberation of the righteous. The Antichrist was an apocalyptic motif connected then with the loosening of Satan and a collective anguish that anticipated a renewal of divine leadership.

Spanish apocalyptic motifs were, as in the rest of Europe, popular during the Middle Ages, and their popularity had continued in spite of successive failed predictions of the end of the world. Those motifs were accentuated by the ideas of apocalypticists like Joachim de Fiore, monastic and secular millenarianism, epidemics, and popular ardency for fatalism. In the thirteenth century, Berceo wrote *Signos que aparecerán antes del Juicio Final*, a narrative poem that listed the fifteen signs that would anticipate Judgment Day. Different narratives about these fifteen signs proliferated in Europe and were associated with pre-Christian Sibylline oracles translated at some point into Latin and inserted into various *Signa judicii* (Ramoneda 1980, 22–23). Supposedly echoing a sermon by St. Jerome, Berceo's narrative addresses the social and religious corruption of his time, imploring for penitence and warning that God will see and judge all "en medio del mercado" (in the middle of the marketplace; 1980, 148, line 70).[37]

"Final Judgment" belongs to the tradition of homiletic and visionary apocalypticism. It is a general exhortation to remember the sins committed and to repent, to revise religious allegiances, and to accept the destiny that Christian divinity affords at the final judgment. The drama is also an allegorization of New Spanish paganism that deploys significant aspects of Christian instruction such as respect for the sacraments of matrimony, penitence, and confession and for the notions of death and the Church as promoted by Tridentine Catholicism.

Although individualized by sins and gender, the Nahua character of Lucía may represent neophytes who have not converted, who have only partially converted, or who have already embraced as lawful the Christian liturgy. The friars measured catechization at any level, we must recall, in terms of expressions of devotion and daily participation in Christian ritual practices, whether they knew them to be genuine or not. In this drama, abstract symbols adopt recognizable human (Nahua) faces resulting in a simple and categorical vision of a final tribulation.

The drama begins with wind instruments to indicate the use of music, "Heaven will open" to refer to the manipulation of space and to signal a spatial hierarchy, and ends with "Saint Michael will descend" to confirm the hierarchy but also to acknowledge a metaphysical distinction. Saint Michael comes from above, and a Nahua audience would therefore perceive him as a messenger of a divinity. The archangel's address, resembling the functional *loa* or introductory address of Spanish *autos*, is equally appealing:

> O creations of God! May you know, and indeed *you already know, for it is in the sacred commands*, that he will finish off, he will destroy the world that his precious and honored father, God, made. He will destroy, he will finish off all that he made, the various birds, the various living creatures, along with you. He will destroy you, you people of the world. But be certain that the dead will revive. The good and proper ones who served the just judge, the sentencer, God, he will take to his royal home, the place of eternal and utter bliss, glory, the place of utter bliss of all the male and female saints. But the bad ones who did not serve our lord God, may they be certain that they will merit suffering in the place of the dead. So then, weep, *remember it*. (1r; my emphasis).

The emphasis on remembering highlights several issues of Franciscan perception of the Nahua. It accentuates doctrine taught on a constant basis and reemphasizes the idea that the Nahua had a partial knowledge of God's laws, a suggestion much encouraged in ecclesiastical sixteenth-century chronicles of New Spain. In particular, it was important to place these notions in a context of remembrance. From Gonzalo Fernández de Oviedo (1478–1557), among other chroniclers, we know that the natives had a special capacity to memorize "las cosas pasadas e antiguas" (past and ancient things; 113–14).[38]

By presenting a Nahua audience with this idea of remembrance, the drama is also trying to generate parallels between some religious predispositions and Christian doctrine. The drama is not, in fact, giving the impression of teaching something new but is trying to help the audience evoke a knowledge many of the evangelists assumed natives already had. The "you already know" of the exhortation's beginning signals a different act of remembrance from the decree of the end, "remember." The two could be complementary, however, in the sense that both acts direct attention to recalling and then maintaining a covenant.

Arróniz ventures an interpretation that deserves consideration, although it may, in a superficial sense, assign too much importance to the friars' campaign without recognizing also the active role played by the Nahua in translating the new doctrine. From the reports given by different chronicles, we have gathered that the drama caused much commotion and excitement among the audience. We have also come to recognize in these descriptions a Franciscan fervor that crystallized often in hyperbolic descriptions of conversion and optimism. At the same time, we should keep in mind that spectacles like this and "The Conquest of Jerusalem" may have been large-scale productions that involved on occasion local settings and more often than not collective participation. In this light, Arróniz wonders what in "Final Judgment" could have caused such excitement and wonderment in the natives of Tlatelolco (1979, 20).

As Arróniz discerns, the exemplary nature of the drama served to instill terror toward a God who was inflexible—in this case about unmarried promiscuity. We should remember that the drama is named *Nexcuitilmachiotl*, a word derived in part from *nexcuitilli* meaning "example we take from others," and not from *temachiyotiliztli*, which means "example we give to others" (Molina 1977, 96v). This semantic distinction in Nahuatl between exemplary agent and target, Arróniz argues, was indicative of a people used to ritualizing victory and defeat (1979, 22). As a continuation of examples of victory, "Final Judgment," then, promotes a model to be first evoked, adopted, and remembered.

The personifications of Penance, Time, and Death continue to emphasize remembrance. First, Penance denounces all world inhabitants for their sins *(intlatlacol)*, which they are unable to avoid (1v). Accusations that prophesy death follow this admonition, denouncing how blind and deaf the Nahua are, and lament their forgetfulness of God (1v). It is Time who next pronounces itself a herald of God and reminds the audience (we imagine a very dramatic and authoritative appeal) of their need to remember God and to show remorse and serve Him: "I am crying out into their ears so that they will remember their creator, their maker, the deity, the ruler, God" (2r). Time's words echo Saint Michael's earlier mention of the coming of the Last Judgment and inculcate again the importance of recollection, of summoning Nahua past actions in order to face God's Judgment. Holy Church then takes the general calling for remembrance and redirects it around the sacrament of matrimony, appealing to the audience to cry and feel remorse.

Sweeping continues, declaiming that many of the Nahua have yet to confess or have not confessed in sufficient measure.[39] The emphasis is again on recollection, on rendering an account of "how they lived on earth" (3r). This mental collection of so-called sinful actions took many forms as the friars tried to promote the belief that much of Nahua ritual life was defiled. We recall Motolinia's description of some early attempts at extracting confessions, in which the Nahua would bring "escriptos" (writings) of their sins (1996, 261). Many of these participants were, Motolinia explains, Nahua women married to Spaniards. He also commends the Indians for their willingness to discipline themselves by public flagellation (260). Self-disciplining occurred frequently too, every Friday, and during Lent three days a week (260). Sweeping's urging for penitence, fasting, and purification of heart assumed that, in the natives' memories, there were fresh references of Christian commendation and instruction.

Death closes the circle of exhortation begun by Penance by making the first reference to hell, which the friars often translated as *mictlan* in Nahuatl, the place where the sinful will fall. Sahagún is known to have questioned the adoption of certain Nahua terms to translate Christian notions to the natives. He insisted that *tlacatecolotl*, another term used to translate "diablo," was inadequate although it referred to necromancy, apparitions, and the underworld (1990, 1:267).[40]

Burkhart has argued, using as an example the lack of such references in Sahagún, that some friars were less inclined to read eschatological signs in New Spain. They concentrated, instead, on daily observances (1989, 82). Individual salvation remains a more common theme, with the Nahua's "collective orientation," Burkhart explains, "focus[ing] upon patron saints and community festivals" (82). Daily observances called for purification and cleansing of hearts, although not in as strident a fashion as that of "Final Judgment." In the drama, the appeal acquires an immediate dramatic referent with the appearance of Lucía, an Indian woman verisimilar enough to represent an individual case while maintaining the metonymic value suggested by a collective responsibility.

Lucía appears when Death and Confession leave the stage accompanied by the sound of trumpets. She makes an entrance announcing how distraught she is at the coming of Judgment and how she needs to be confessed (4r–v). The character of Lucía could signal a converted or partially converted member of the Nahua community whose sacramental behavior has been partial to Christian doctrine, suggesting, as many Nahua believed, that a confessor could remedy this imbalance and help to purify the defiled person.

In the drama, the priest and confessor reacts with much exasperation, and his imprecations to Lucía serve only to heighten the sense of doom. He expresses how terrible—"four hundred times"—are the sins committed by Lucía and how the devil is responsible for her distancing herself from God and from the sacrament of matrimony (4v). Lucía is left alone, recognizing her terrible sin. She repents to save her life, albeit too late, calling herself a great sinner.

Portrayed as a false god, Antichrist appears, raising a left hand and wearing a "mantle of wickedness." He speaks to his "children" and then vanishes while fireworks proclaim the entrance of Christ. The directions describe the opening of the skies as Christ descends in the company of Saint Michael, who is carrying the scales of justice. After the singing of "Christus Factus Est," Christ declares the end of the world in terms of cleansing: "As I set down in my sacred commands, I will sweep things, I will purify heaven and earth" (6r).

The drama continues with the gathering of the living and the dead and a continuation of Lucía's condemnation before Christ. Categorical condemnation extends to other characters among the living and the dead, who are brought in by Saint Michael. As the condemned enter, devils torture and pester them. Christ interrogates each one in connection with the sacraments (matrimony, for Lucía), proclaiming punishment and reminding them of the torment they will endure. This torment, Christ proclaims, includes also a type of recollection of sins and vices that will be paraded before her (8r–v).

By linking Lucía's religious affiliation with service to earthly vices, Christ is presenting this as a crucial cause of her proscription. Because this is a physical act of eviction, it may recall the myth of expulsion from Eden, a theme many evangelized Nahua knew in some variety. The Nahua, personified here by Lucía, are reminded of Edenic life via accounting of transgressions. The "perfect symbol for centrality and order" often associated by the friars with the Nahua "heaven" *Tlalocan* (Burkhart 1989, 70) becomes indirectly an instrument of coercion. Lucía's late recognition is met with violence and torture, as she faces demons who push her violently into a steaming hell.

Instead of the word *mictlan*, the composite expression *temazcalli* is used here to designate this place of suffering.[41] Sahagún explains that the *temazcalli* was associated with the curing of diseases and with the cleansing of impurities (1990, 1:461, 2:904). The friars may have tried to link the curative symbolism of the *temazcalli* with the purgatorial elements usually associated with hell and purgatory, an association that could extend to the *tlachpanaliztli* that promotes cleansing and confession. Although *mictlan* was not a place of fire, fire played prominently in the ritual of the New Fire, which celebrated a new calendar round. Fire was related intimately with the gods Huitzilopochtli and Tezcatlipoca, reported obsessively by the friars as horrible manifestations of the devil.

It is difficult to know what kind of perception the audience entertained when these associations of Nahua symbols and Christian valuations intermingled. The New Fire ritual of renewal included certainly a fear of destruction and a great anxiety that translated into a multiplicity of wondrous expectations (such as, pregnant women turning into animals, for example; Burkhart 1989, 73). To mention fire in connection with hell—a house of torture and pain—was surely an unintended attempt to mix preconquest and Christian manifestations of dread. The devils may have been perceived as *tzitzimime* as well, in the event that the ritual of the New Fire did not draw fire: "If fire could not be drawn, then the Tzitzimime would descend from the heavens to consume humankind" (Miller and Taube 1993, 87).[42] Like the *tzitzimime*, the devils in "Final Judgment" may have suggested supernatural characteristics and the power to "consume," as alimentary metaphors become manifest in their speech.

Perhaps this is what Second Demon and Satan imply, after several demons gather instruments of torture:

Second Demon: Grab up the fiery chains and the fiery metal staff with which we will beat them and tell our ruler, Lucifer, that we are taking his servants over there. Let him quickly send the fiery metal warping frame there where we will take his servants.

Satan: I am bringing everything right here with which we will tie them up so that not one will flee from our hands. *Now we have our drink and our food,* there in the depths of the place of the dead. We exerted all our efforts so that our servants fell into our hands. (8v–9r; my emphasis)

The insinuation is that devils can devour their victims, an act that could easily summon images of *tzitzimime* under certain changes in the skies, such as solar eclipses. The *tzitzimime* were also thought to descend headfirst from above (Miller and Taube 1993, 176), a belief the friars may have echoed in New Spanish iconography of the devil. Examples of descending devils abound in medieval iconography. Illustrations of this iconography in New Spain appeared in open chapels and churches and were surely replicated in iconography and plays. Plates 8 and 10 of Muñoz Camargo's *Descripción de la ciudad y provincia de Tlaxcala* also give an idea of the type of iconography that informed the plays in general. Devils resemble medieval devils as either descending on Christian icons (plate 8) or running from fire (plate 10). The devils in the drama play a role that promotes fear of pain and agony, using images that have, moreover, strong preconquest associations.

"Final Judgment" dramatizes scenes taken from biblical scripture, and it probably epitomizes in New Spain—granted we understand the collective staging of the drama in the context of massive didacticism—the *sensus allegoricus* Zumthor identifies with medieval religious drama. Most of the medieval drama that revolved around the cosmic struggle between God and the devil, Zumthor argues, implied a figuration of the two (1972, 438).[43] The devils belong to the array of characters the friars tried to associate with preconquest apparitions (of priests, of supernatural beings, for example) and to the cosmology of an anti-Christian world that threatens to substitute Christian worship and *ordo*. It may be that this event of the Last Judgment was for the Nahua just another *prodigio*, a portent with no sweeping importance beyond the spectacular.

At this point, it would be fitting to conclude with Muñoz Camargo's description of *prodigios* (portents) from his *Historia de Tlaxcala*. He explains how the native Tlaxcalans responded to events that carried eschatological symbolism. Referring to the sign of fire that would mark an end to the world, with a ball of fire and universal death, Muñoz Camargo retells how the Nahua interpreted the arrival of the Spanish to be precisely this sign. He ventures the following account:

> Tienen por muy cierto que ha de haber otro fin, que ha de ser por fuego y que la tierra ha de tragarse a los hombres, que todo el universo mundo se ha de abrasar y que han de bajar del cielo los dioses y las estrellas, que, personalmente, han de destruir a los hombres del mundo y acaballos, y que las estrellas han de venir en figuras salvajes. Este es el último fin que ha de haber en el mundo. Cuando los nuestros llegaron a esta provincia, como atrás lo dejaremos tratado, entendieron que era llegado el fin del mundo, según las señales y apariencias tan claras que veían.

> They hold as true that there will be another end, that it will come in fire and that the earth will swallow humankind, that the entire universe will be in flames and that gods and stars will descend from heaven. They will destroy all humans, will finish them off, and the stars will resemble savage figures. This is the last end in the world. When our ancestors arrived to this province, as was explained earlier in this treatise, they perceived that it was the end of the world, according to the clear signs and apparitions they saw. (1986, 170–71)

According to Muñoz Camargo, these signs of calamity provoked dread and concern and occasioned collective expressions of pain, cries, and rituals of bloodletting (180). We must still wonder what type of response Nahua catechumens had to the devotional and apocalyptic motifs that the friars, and especially the Franciscans, popularized. Certainly, a changed consciousness of renewal and of end times may have settled in, and Judgment Day played a role in that readjustment. Perhaps for the Nahua this cognitive process of reading apocalyptic signs was in some fundamental ways similar to that of a medieval member of the laity. The medieval mind read visually when confronted with a text, as Bevington explains, and "textually in terms of narrative and moral lesson, when confronted with an image" (1975, 6).

"Final Judgment" was the text and subtext that the friars were constantly teaching to the Nahua in sacramental practices, in the primitive liturgy of catechism, and its power derived from persistent visual reading. Its exemplary nature and its didacticism came after the visual fact. The need to designate the territory of conflictual reality, as it becomes manifest in the geography of texts I have studied, is unavoidable. "Nahuatized Christianity" certainly favors the belief in a Nahua active response whereby Christianity was reformulated along with Nahua beliefs, generating what could aptly be termed popular Christianities. The deployment of Christian doctrine meant to instill a belief in inherited defilement and to "amend" cultural traditions of self and society. As Adorno discerns, Amerindian peoples learned from discourses of sin and the Commandments a social code of behavior that helped to determine relations between races, dominant and dominated (1990, 31). And yet, Nahuatl drama reverberated in many other experiences of Christian dogma such as miracles, exempla, and anecdotes—stories and modes of telling that gave birth to multiple experiences and perceptions of Christian doctrine, toppling the millenarian expectation of a homogeneous Christian state.

Notes

1. The adequacy of the qualifier "catechistic" for Nahuatl drama may draw some attention. That didactic and Christian elements present in Nahuatl drama tried to promote specific ideas and types of behavior consonant with Catholic indoctrination is not a matter of dispute. However, a distinction must be drawn between specific texts or performances that were grafted onto the evolving identity of a community and those that had an initial catechistic intention. When some of the *autos* were first introduced, they had, we assume, specific objectives besides bringing as many neophytes together as possible: the teaching of sacramental practices (marriage, confession) and other aspects of Christian doctrine such as belief in the Devil, Hell, defilement by sin, divine intervention (as in miracles) and punishment, to name a few. The continuation of these performances resulted eventually in the reenactment of dramas

whose proselytizing goal was no longer a primary attribute. Needs to reassert local cults, to please or appease local divinities (or saints), and perhaps even to excel in both presentation and importance of the *altepetl* or the community, may have infused the performances with much distinctiveness.

2. Dramatizations of catechistic and edifying plays must have started as early as the 1530s (Ricard 1966, 195; Horcasitas 1974, 562–63; Burkhart 1989, 80). Fernando Horcasitas had a pioneering interest in Nahuatl drama and his published volume *El teatro náhuatl* (1974) gathered an impressive array of examples. The second volume, yet to be published, is now under the guidance of Dr. María Sten in Mexico City. With the publication of Louise Burkhart's *Holy Wednesday* (1996) and the advent of new research on devotional material using Nahuatl sources, there has been renewed interest in Nahuatl drama. For a compressed bibliography on work done on Nahuatl theater, consult Burkhart 1996 (281–82). Vivid although probably suspect descriptions of the plays come from the early friars such as Motolinia and Las Casas. Chimalpahin mentions that in 1533 there was in Santiago of Tlatelolco a representation *(neyxcuitilli)* of the end of the world (1998, 2:187) and mentions Passion plays being represented in 1583 and 1587 in Mexico City (2:257, 263). More *representaciones* are mentioned in other Nahua chronicles. I will revisit these descriptions later in the essay.

3. My use of the phrase "popular Christianity" in reference to colonial Mexico will be explored below.

4. By "radicalized" is here meant the permutation undergone by any cultural model in the process of becoming, consciously or not, a defining instrument of identity. In a concrete sense, the term is linked with the semantics of root or "rooting," which would connote also a process of making something a foundation, a base, in a sense of inhabiting and appropriating a space. In Spanish the verb *radicar* means also to be the inhabitant of a place. In the case of colonial Mexico, the situation is especially complicated by the diversity of agents and motives acting upon a "knowledge" presumed by the friars and church officials to be unchangeable and homogenizing; and also by the different degrees and nature of catechesis. Nahuas, it appears, accepted Christian ways mostly as a means to order, reorder, and preserve what to them were acceptable and Nahua-consonant lifestyles, in spite of the various displacements they underwent after the conquest (Lockhart 1992, 208; 1991, 10). At the same time, Nahuas preserved many of the core traditions of official religiosity. One must wonder what the pope would see if he visited a church in a local Tzotzil community in Chiapas, whether his unspoken discomfort with popular Catholicism would find reconciliation only in the numbers.

5. This is by no means an original idea. The background Burkhart lays out in *Holy Wednesday* (1996, 14–36) opens up a wide range of interpretations and possibilities, calling for an appraisal of Nahuatl drama that emphasizes Nahua agency (42–48): "Colonial Nahuatl theater was a literary and performance genre that developed separately from Spanish colonial drama. Plays were performed in the Nahuatl language, by Nahua authors, and for a principally Nahua audience" (42). Her belief that Nahuatl drama resembles biblical and hagiographic earlier Spanish *autos* rather than Golden Age *comedias* and *autos sacramentales* (42) is by now indisputable. Luis Weckmann has also discussed issues of continuity in his seminal work on the medieval heritage in Mexico, also in the context of popular religiosity (1984, 248–72).

6. The most often cited work is Robert Ricard's *La "conquête spirituelle" du Mexique* (1933; published in English in 1966), an influential work in ecclesiastical history stressing the belief that the Christian campaign had been for the most part, if equivocal in some cases, still a successful and sweeping endeavor. His interpretation relied heavily on the accounts of the early friars, some of whom, like fray Toribio Motolinia, fray Bernardino de Sahagún, and fray Andrés de Olmos, had developed an extensive knowledge of Nahua culture, language, and history. This interpretation has found echoes in many other works, including Georges Baudot's *Utopie et histoire au Mexique* (1976). See Sarah Cline's "The Spiritual Conquest Reexamined" (2000), Lockhart (1992, 2–6), Klor de Alva (1982, 345; 1993, 175), and Burkhart (1996, 59–61) for reassessments and critiques of Ricard's interpretation.

7. The term *folkloric* has had a variety of uses and may not be adequate to designate Mesoamerican civilizations with complex and sophisticated religious, political, and social

systems, lest we be faulted for romanticizing Nahua responses to religious colonialism. The same caution would apply to the term *popular culture,* which even Gurevich has limited to the early Middle Ages, "when the overwhelming majority of the population were peasants and their style of thinking necessarily affected the totality of social consciousness" (1993, xix). The equation of popular and Nahuatized Christianity is a qualitative and useful one, however. *Popular* is neither conceived as a vulgarized version of Christianity (a prejudice that has determined much medieval scholarship to this day) nor is *Nahuatized* seen as a partial or primitive expression of it. I would like to ask for the reader's indulgence in the hope that this analogy will later become clearer. To my understanding, the term *Nahuatized* was first developed by Klor de Alva, under the premise that Christianity for the Nahua meant a continuation rather than a break of their own religion(s) (1993, 175). The idea of Nahuatization, however, is evident in earlier works by Lockhart and Burkhart.

8. Most of the texts written in Nahuatl were made up of doctrines, confessionaries and catechisms, and what we could term casuistry guides. Ruiz de Alarcón's treatise on superstitions written in 1629 may be considered one such guide, meant to catalog the perceptions and practices that its future readers intended to change or eradicate. For studies of Nahuatl printed books, see Ascensión H. de León-Portilla's *Tepuztlahcuilolli: Impresos en náhuatl: Historia y bibliografía* (1988), Barry D. Sell's *Friars, Nahuas, and Books: Language and Expression in Colonial Nahuatl Publications* (1993), and "The Classical Age of Nahuatl Publications and Don Bartolomé de Alva's *Confessionario* of 1634" (Sell and Schwaller 1999). Sell 1993 includes a listing of books by genre.

9. An earlier version of this text was first published in 1990 in *Estudios de Cultura Náhuatl* 20.

10. Sahagún, and later Molina, were known to have had problems with the translation of doctrinal material, although fray Maturino Gilberti's seventeen-year trial (1559–1576)—because of his translation into Tarascan of the *Diálogos de doctrina cristiana*—has been more widely documented (Ricard 1966, 58–60).

11. This predicament of the Spanish ecclesiastical authorities was by no means ever settled. In the eighteenth century, fray Benito Jerónimo Feijóo was still writing about the need to control religious festivities in his *Teatro crítico universal* (vol. 6, para. 2): "La multitud de días festivos, perjudicial al interés de la República, y nada conveniente a la Religión (On the plethora of feasts, harmful to the Republic, and not at all suitable to Religion). Advocating control over the "abusos" and "profanaciones" that had so much infiltrated religious festivities, Feijóo presents a summarized account of many of the Councils, especially in Spain, that dealt with this issue, including the Council of Cambray (1565) and Burdeos (1583) (6:147–52).

12. The texts of the *Junta de 1544* and the *Concilio Provincial Mexicano* of 1555, 1565, and 1585 appear reprinted in Llaguno's *La personalidad jurídica del indio y el III Concilio Provincial Mexicano (1585)* (1962). This and subsequent translations are mine, unless otherwise noted.

13. "Las representaciones teatrales de la Pasión," *Boletín del Archivo General de la Nación* (1934): 332–56. Louise Burkhart informed me that this case had in fact been documented in the *Boletín*. The volume of *Fondo Inquisición* from which this text was extracted is 1182. I located a similar though more extensive description of this incident in volume 1072, folios 195–294. A friend in Mexico informed me that the case the *Boletín* transcribes (dated June 18, 1770) is a summarized account of the 1768 case. The 1934 paleography includes a portion of a play dealing with Pontius Pilate's dictate after the Jews have condemned Jesus, but it does not offer transcriptions of full-length confiscated passion plays that appear at the end of the 1768 corpus I identified. Horcasitas relies on the *Boletín*'s 1934 publication for his short analysis (1974, 425–30). On eighteenth-century Passion plays of presumed earlier Nahua authorship, see Juan Leyva's *La Pasión de Ozumba,* a compact and well-researched study and edition of one of two Ozumba Passion plays taken from the plays confiscated by the Inquisition in 1768. This inci-dent deserves further scrutiny in the hope of shedding more light on the dynamics of Nahua Christian religiosity as it evolved into the eighteenth century. A full study of the case, including paleography of the plays, is under preparation for future publication.

14. *Archivo General de la Nación,* Fondo Tierras, vol. 2778, exp. 2, 25 (1680).

15. The famous *coloquios* attributed to Sahagún and his Nahua aides was subjected to revisions ("limóse") in order to reflect an exchange more or less determined by the catechistic zeal (Sahagún 1986, 20).

16. From Nahuatl *tlaca(tl)* (person) and *huapahu(a)* (to raise children) (Karttunen 1992, 81, 253; Molina 1977, 116r). No longer the only rendering from Nahuatl, "Tlacahuapahualiztli" has been translated here as "How to Live on Earth." It was translated by John H. Cornyn and Byron McAfee as "Bringing Up Children," a translation followed by Ravicz. Both McAfee and Cornyn place its conception and possible performance after the fall of the capital of Moctezuma, between 1521 and 1530 (316); whereas Horcasitas, who translated the title as "La educación de los hijos," believes it was conceived and performed between 1540 and 1550 (1974, 79). One of the play's themes is the disposition of material goods after death, which indicates prolonged exposure to Spanish ecclesiastical and legal proceedings and expectations concerning the aftermath of death. The first decade after the arrival of the twelve Franciscans is surely too early for this play to have been written or enacted.

17. Translation courtesy of Louise Burkhart. Translations of dramas discussed in this essay are courtesy of Louise Burkhart and Barry Sell and can be found in this volume.

18. Our knowledge of the myth of the Fall in Nahuatl drama starts with "La caída de nuestros primeros padres" (The Fall of Our First Parents), although earlier ideographic renderings were certainly used to transmit the story. According to Motolinia, this *auto* was performed outdoors by native Tlaxcalans honoring the feast of Easter. The Tlaxcalans assisted Cortés in his victory over the Mexicans and in the occupation of Moctezuma's city in 1521. Motolinia described a performance of this play in his *Historia de los Indios de la Nueva España* (1985, 200-202). García Icazbalceta published this and other descriptions appearing in Motolinia in his "Representaciones religiosas de México en el siglo XVI" (1968, 313-37). There are short references to this drama in Las Casas, who cites Motolinia's description (1967, 1:329-31), and in Torquemada (1986, 3:231); but they do not contribute any new information. Horcasitas has shown that the dialogue partially resembles one found in the *Doctrina cristiana en lengua española y mexicana por los religiosos de la orden de Santo Domingo* (1548) (Horcasitas 1974, 176, 179-83). Not much else can be derived from other sources.

19. Early Christian and medieval books of penance (some of which acquired differing shapes in the New World in the form of catechisms and confessionaries) were employed in facilitating a transition from paganism to Christianity; they provided, as well, an ordered and elaborate series of questions and descriptions with the intention of regulating religious and social behavior (McNeill and Gamer 1990, 3). The "Penitential of Silos," which describes penalties for and descriptions of sacramental and social transgressions, is a good Spanish example (285-90). Penitentials existed therefore to exercise control, which would in turn ensure the purification of the Christian community (Tentler 1977, 12). Braswell points out that in many ways the medieval sinner stood alone, in isolation, at least until confession was ended and an order had been issued to do penance and "sin no more" (1983, 13). An interesting difference arises between the medieval sinner, whose sense of collectivity in sin comes only by way of sharing a doctrinal and sacramental knowledge with others, and the Nahua sinner, who had to simultaneously internalize this knowledge, redefining the nature and context of transgression, and to realize his or her position in the face of authority, penitence, and the reestablishment of order.

20. Horcasitas believes that some of these dramas were directed at both colonizers and colonized alike, emphasizing different aspects of didacticism (1974, 170). In my view, this drama belongs to the didactic representations in the tradition of the seven sins, with direct admonitory intentions directed in this case primarily at the natives: to teach retribution and repentance of specific sins in the context of Christian salvation, with a clear emphasis on the symbolic value, or lack thereof, of material goods and property.

21. As Bevington explains in his prologue to "Everyman," however, Good Deeds refers not only to a series of charitable acts that will pave the way to salvation and grace, but also to issues affecting the Church, such as the prescription of proper penitential rites and scourging (1975, 939).

22. Personifications of abstractions were very popular in pre-Renaissance Spanish drama, evident in the variety and number present in the "autos viejos." Catechistic drama presents few examples, of which Holy Church, Death, Penance, and Sweeping each make a salient appearance, all in the apocalyptic drama "Juicio Final." Some of the names of these personifications differ from Horcasitas's translation (1974, 561–93), where Confession and Penitence are used instead.

23. Translation of this play courtesy of Barry Sell.

24. For a view of the historical context of the sacrament of penitence and the dogma of sins, see Lu Ann Homza's article "The European Link to Mexican Penance" (1999).

25. See, for instance, the "Oración del Padre Nuestro en jeroglífico," published in Cuevas 1928, 1:186.

26. Observing days of penance (as in fasts), along with hearing mass, and going to confession at least once a year—all these were part of the Precepts of the Church, or Commandments of the Church.

27. The idea of guilt as a contractual construct has been identified in connection with practices of penance, particularly in the context of the medieval Christian world. Mary C. Mansfield, for instance, finds similar associations in thirteenth-century France: "Penance in the most general sense was obviously about reconciliation: the payment of a moral debt, the restoration of social relations, the reinstatement of the excommunicant, the renewal of peace" (1994, 289). Maureen Flynn's essay "The Spectacle of Suffering in Spanish Streets" connects this retributive "exchange" in terms of the body, and its capacity symbolically to transfer its suffering and pain, "circulating as a costly currency in the purchase of spiritual goods" (1994, 161).

28. Translation courtesy of Barry Sell. Fernando Horcasitas speculates that the creation or performance of this play occurred between 1540 and 1550 (1974, 79). This drama is one of the most apocalyptic of all, along with "Final Judgment." Although its main subject is the teaching of respect for the dead and the Christian notion of purgatorial suffering in connection with the prayers and honoring for the dead (by way of masses, etc.), it encompasses didactic material such as it is found in *Doctrinas* (for example, the Sacraments and the Ten Commandments, a Last Judgment scene with a wheel of fire, and an underworld).

29. Another play, entitled "The Life of Don Sebastián," also introduces the Commandments at the end of the play. In "Souls and Testamentary Executors," this exchange occurs between Saint Michael and Lucifer, whereas in "The Life of Don Sebastián" it is between personified Death and Lucifer and several demons. Saint Michael presents them as commands whereas Death interrogates one of the demons.

30. In her commentary on this drama, Ravicz discusses why a woman, and not a man, is the protagonist of chastisement and reckoning. She believes it was easier to present a woman as a symbol of negative values since "the fear of God and divine retribution is traditionally more easily instilled into women than men" (1970, 233). Although she makes no mention of the extension of medieval Christian misogyny and the tradition of portraying women as "naturally" weaker and as instruments of the devil, Ravicz does present the possibility that some of the evangelistic dramas used women as protagonists in some instances because, in Nahua culture, women had a certain responsibility in the instruction of children and in the preservation of sanctity in the home (1970, 233–34). Lucía in "Final Judgment," Hagar in "The Sacrifice of Isaac," and Widow in "Souls and Testamentary Executors" are vivid portrayals of this possible meaning.

31. Any student of colonial historiography must acknowledge also certain Nahua interpretations. Initially, one responds to New World narratives with a certain incredulity, finding a range of gestures that often smack of absurdity. Muñoz Camargo confirms that many natives had precisely this kind of response when they saw the friars preach: "Cuando predicaban estas cosas, decían los señores caciques: 'Qué han estos pobres miserables? Mirad si tienen hambre y, si han menester algo, dadles de comer'" (When they preached these things, the lord chiefs said: "What is the matter with these miserable beggars? See if they are hungry and, if they want something, feed them"; 1986, 177). Other Indian nobles and priests identified those foreign gestures simply as signs of sickness or madness: "Estos pobres deben de ser enfermos o estar

locos. Dejadlos vocear a los miserables, tomádoles a su mal de locura. Dejadlos estar [y] que pasen su enfermedad como pudieren" (These beggars must be sick or mad. Let them rave, such poor people with their madness, and let them deal with their sickness however they may; 1986, 177). The newcomers, carriers of wondrous words and objects, often seemed to the Nahua in need of attention.

32. Its first line, "Nexcuitilmachiotl motenehua juiçio final," translates into "Exemplary sign called Final Judgment." Below, the lines "y tetlatzontequilizylhuitl" provide another reference to the Day of Judgment (Horcasitas 1974, 564). Translations of this play are courtesy of Louise Burkhart.

33. Eschatological themes appear in several other dramas, such as the several *autos* and *farsas* on the Resurrection (Rouanet 1979, 4:66, 3:1, 2:514) and Adam and Eve (4:1, 2:133, 216, 243) Even *farsas sacramentales* such as "Desafío del hombre" (challenge of man; 3:513) echo eschatological sentiments, as a worried Church declares that man's prayer and penitence, with God's guidance, are needed for salvation (3:527). Prayer and Penitence are also characters in this play, in conflict with Lucifer, Lies, and Pride. Another interesting example is "Farsa sacramental de la residencia del hombre" (sacramental farce about man's residence [on earth]), in which Man comes before Justice and Conscience to be sentenced for his sins (1:153–54).

34. The myth of Xochiquetzal was associated with Eve in Eden, and echoes of Noah and the biblical flood were identified with floods of a previous Nahua age (Burkhart 1989, 77).

35. See Burkhart's article in this volume. Her study of the dramas and translations provides a clear and general idea of how the Nahua understood death and how catechistic drama attempted to reorient perceptions and responses to this final event, legally, socially, and theologically.

36. Historians have referred to "Final Judgment" at different lengths. Garibay speaks of a "Juicio Universal," a drama performed supposedly in 1535 that he, like García Icazbalceta, attributes to Olmos, who had arrived in New Spain in 1528 (1987, 2:131). Garibay believes this "Juicio" to be the same as the twenty-one-page manuscript located at the Library of Congress, the same on which Horcasitas bases his translation into Spanish. Horcasitas is one of the first to study this drama in some detail and to provide a summary of what the early chroniclers wrote (1974, 562–67). John Cornyn and Byron McAfee's 1932 translation was published in Ravicz's *Early Colonial Religious Drama in Mexico* in 1970. Othón Arróniz studied the drama in some detail, providing useful interpretations and historical background, in his book *Teatro de evangelización en Nueva España* (1979). In 1992, Jerry Williams published a study of colonial drama in Mexico that deals briefly with this piece (1992, 50–55). Susan McMillen Villar provided a synthetic background of the drama and a more extensive analysis than Horcasitas did, in her dissertation "Drama and the Theater in the Millenarian Project of the Franciscans in New Spain" (1993). The drama is referenced in chronicles and in most historical studies of evangelization in New Spain, which suggests the possibility that several reenactments occurred at least in Tlatelolco and Mexico City between 1531 and 1539.

37. The association of commerce and trade to official religiosity did not escape the watchful eyes of the Mexican councils. Chapter 4 of the Provincial Council of 1555 warns against the "mercados y tianguez" (market places) set up by the natives, on saints' days or on Sundays, because they distracted them and kept them from mass, sermons, and festivities celebrated in their own towns (in Llaguno 1983, 188–69).

38. See Las Casas (1995, 1:23–6; 1967), Motolinia (1985, 113), and Torquemada (3:122) for views about a native pre-Christianity

39. Given that the exhortation here centers on confession, Horcasitas has translated *Tlachpanaliztli* as Confession. Burkhart has opted to maintain the literal meaning of "acto de barrer" (act of sweeping; Molina 1992, 117v) in order to preserve the Nahuatl sense of cleaning.

40. See Burkhart for a discussion of Sahagún's responses to the use of Nahua terms by the friars to designate Christian ideas (1989, 41–45).

41. *Temazcal* is a Hispanicized version of Nahuatl *temazcalli*. Molina identifies this as the name of a kind of public bath, a furnace with vapors where the Nahua bathe or clean themselves (1977:97v).

42. See the discussion above on *chichimicle* or *tzitzimime*, dealing with Martin Ucelo's apocalyptic use of the name in connection with the friars

43. Zumthor's notion of "ordo" derives from his analysis of the *Jeu d'Adam* as *Ordo representaciones Adae*, a name given to the play by the copier (1972, 438). Zumthor's ideas about religious medieval drama ("prédication par personnages" [preaching through characters]) are applicable to catechistic drama in New Spain precisely in the context of allegorization. Allegorization was for the friars both a "réalité ultime" (final reality) and a didactic mechanism that appealed, as in Zumthor's dramatized Scripture or hagiographic *legenda* (legends), to audiences' sensory perceptions (439).